Modern Slavery Legislation

This book will aid understanding and interpretation of the Californian, UK and Australian Modern Slavery Acts, and will provide an in-depth three-way comparative analysis between the three Acts.

Modern slavery is a new legal compliance issue, with new legislation enacted in California (Transparency in Supply Chains Act, 2010), the UK (Modern Slavery Act, 2015) and most recently, Australia (Modern Slavery Act, 2018). Such legislation mandates that business of a certain size annually disclose the steps that they are taking to ensure that modern slavery is not occurring in their own operations and supply chains. The legislation applies to businesses wherever incorporated or formed. Key aspects of primary focus will include lessons learned from the California, UK and Australian experience and central arguments on contentious issues, for example: monetary threshold for determining reporting entities, penalties for non-compliance, compliance lists and appointment of an Anti-Slavery Commissioner. The book will also discuss how contentious issues were ultimately resolved and will undertake a comparative analysis of the Californian, UK and Australian Acts.

Modern Slavery Legislation will be of interest to academics and students of business and human rights law.

Sunil Rao is an international human rights law expert, academic and legal practitioner in the emerging area of regulatory compliance of business supply chains and modern slavery. He is currently Special Counsel at Baker McKenzie and Lecturer at the Law School, La Trobe University. Sunil has previously held the positions of Consultant to UNICEF, Visiting Fellow at the British Institute of International and Comparative Law and Visiting Scholar at the Lauterpacht Centre for International Law, Cambridge University.

Modern Slavery Legislation
Drafting History and Comparisons between Australia, UK and the USA

Sunil Rao

LONDON AND NEW YORK

First published 2020
by Routledge
2 Park Square, Milton Park, Abingdon, Oxon OX14 4RN

and by Routledge
605 Third Avenue, New York, NY 10017

First issued in paperback 2021

Routledge is an imprint of the Taylor & Francis Group, an informa business

Copyright © 2020 Sunil Salankey Rao

The right of Sunil Rao to be identified as author of this work has been asserted by them in accordance with sections 77 and 78 of the Copyright, Designs and Patents Act 1988.

All rights reserved. No part of this book may be reprinted or reproduced or utilised in any form or by any electronic, mechanical, or other means, now known or hereafter invented, including photocopying and recording, or in any information storage or retrieval system, without permission in writing from the publishers.

Trademark notice: Product or corporate names may be trademarks or registered trademarks, and are used only for identification and explanation without intent to infringe.

Publisher's Note
The publisher has gone to great lengths to ensure the quality of this reprint but points out that some imperfections in the original copies may be apparent.

British Library Cataloguing-in-Publication Data
A catalogue record for this book is available from the British Library

Library of Congress Cataloging-in-Publication Data
Names: Rao, Sunil author.
Title: Modern slavery legislation: drafting history and comparisons between Australia, UK and the USA / Sunil Rao.
Description: Abingdon, Oxon; New York, NY: Routledge, 2020. | Includes bibliographical references and index.
Identifiers: LCCN 2019050033 (print) | LCCN 2019050034 (ebook) | ISBN 9780367347789 (hardback) | ISBN 9780429341465 (ebook)
Subjects: LCSH: Forced labor—Law and legislation. | Human trafficking—Law and legislation. | Business logistics—Government policy. | Australia. Modern Slavery Act 2018. | California. Transparency in Supply Chains Act of 2010. | Great Britain. Modern Slavery Act 2015.
Classification: LCC K3268 .R36 2020 (print) | LCC K3268 (ebook) | DDC 342.08/7—dc23
LC record available at https://lccn.loc.gov/2019050033
LC ebook record available at https://lccn.loc.gov/2019050034

ISBN 13: 978-1-03-223932-3 (pbk)
ISBN 13: 978-0-367-34778-9 (hbk)

DOI: 10.4324/9780367347789

Typeset in Times New Roman
by codeMantra

Time is a fallacy
Thy soul in sorrow eternally immerses
Writing simply distracts
For upon time I yearn

Contents

Acknowledgments viii

1 Introduction 1

2 The origins of the disclosure approach: *California Transparency in Supply Chains Act 2010* 10

3 Modern Slavery Act UK: transparency in supply chains provision 30

4 Modern Slavery Act Australia 62

5 International comparisons 93

Index 115

Acknowledgments

My most heartfelt and sincere gratefulness to my family: Narayana and Pramila Rao, Samitha and Sowmya. I am forever profoundly appreciative of your eternal love. Sanchita Abrol, I am deeply thankful, and always will be, for ensuring our souls evermore entwine in reflections of conscious splendour.

1 Introduction

Modern slavery is defined by situations of exploitation that a person cannot refuse or may not leave due to threats, violence, and coercion, abuse of power or deception. Modern slavery is practised in a variety of ways, including human trafficking, slavery, practices similar to slavery (including forced labour and forced marriage) and the worst forms of child labour.

Modern slavery persists all over the world, implicating every region and economy, regardless of whether they are industrialised, developing or in transition.[1] A complex and often hidden crime that crosses borders, sectors and jurisdictions, the highest prevalence is in Africa, followed by Asia Pacific, then Europe and Central Asia, the Arab States and the Americas.[2]

There are an estimated 40.3 million men, women and children living in modern slavery at any given moment – 24.9 million forced to work against their will and 15.4 million living in a marriage they didn't agree to.[3] Of those in forced labour, 16 million are compelled to work in the private sector, 4.8 million are in forced sexual exploitation and 4.1 million are in state-imposed forced labour.[4]

Around 57% of the 16 million people in the private sector forced labour are female and 43% are male. One in five are children who either work alone or with their parents.[5] Here, prevalence varies slightly

---

1 Walk Free Foundation, 'Harnessing the Power of Business to End Modern Slavery' (Report, 2018) 7 (*'Harnessing Power of Business'*).
2 International Labour Office, 'Global Estimates of Modern Slavery: Forced Labour and Forced Marriage' (Report, 2017) 10, 26.
3 Ibid 9–10.
4 Ibid 10.
5 Ibid 32.

2 *Introduction*

across the regions. Asia Pacific accounts for the highest prevalence,[6] followed by Europe and Central Asia, then Africa, the Arab States and the Americas.[7]

Almost a quarter (24%) are domestic workers, 18% are in construction, 15% in manufacturing and 11% agriculture and fishing.[8] Male victims are more likely to be in mining, manufacturing, construction and agriculture, while female victims are more likely to be in accommodation and food services and domestic work.[9]

Most forced labour victims are threatened and coerced by their employers or recruiters in multiple ways. Almost a quarter have their wages withheld or have been threatened with this, 17% have been threatened with violence, 16% have experienced physical violence, 12% have received threats against family and 7% of female victims endure sexual violence.[10]

Male victims are more likely to receive threats against family, have wages withheld, be physically confined, denied food and sleep, or be threatened with legal action.[11] Female victims experience higher rates of sexual violence and are more likely to have their passports taken away.[12]

The US Department of Labor's most recent *List of Goods Produced by Child Labor or Forced Labor* contains 148 goods that are made by child or forced labour in 76 countries.[13]

In the agriculture sector, the top two goods produced using forced or child labour are sugarcane and cotton. In the manufacturing industry, bricks and clothes are at the top, while in mining, it's gold and coal.[14]

Brazil, India and Paraguay each have 24 goods produced by forced or child labour, the highest in the world. Among the goods listed are bananas and beef in Brazil, matches and rice in India, and lettuce and limestone in Paraguay.[15]

---

6 Ibid 10.
7 Ibid 10. In absolute numbers, the Asia Pacific region has 64% of victims in forced labour exploitation.
8 Ibid 32.
9 Ibid 33.
10 Ibid 11, 35.
11 Ibid 35.
12 Ibid 35.
13 US Department of Labour, 'List of Goods Produced by Child Labour or Forced Labour' (Report, 2018) 8.
14 Ibid 16.
15 Ibid 8–10.

Introduction 3

The international framework places human rights standards on business based commonly on six main standards: OECD Guidelines for Multinational Enterprises; OECD Due Diligence Guidance for Responsible Supply Chains;[16] United Nations Guiding Principles on Business and Human Rights; United Nations Global Compact Principles; International Organization for Standardization standards;[17] and the Tripartite Declaration of Principles Concerning Multinational Enterprises and Social Policy.

This group of separate, but related, principles are consistent, complementary, mutually-supportive and occasionally linked, and they have a common commitment to human rights.[18]

16 In particular, Organisation for Economic Cooperation and Development, 'Due Diligence Guidance for Responsible Supply Chains in the Garment and Footwear Sector' (OECD, 2017) (*'Due Diligence for Garment and Footwear Sector'*); Organisation for Economic Cooperation and Development and Food and Agriculture Organization of the United Nations, 'Guidance for Responsible Agricultural Supply Chains' (OECD-FAO, 2016) (*'Guidance for Agriculture'*); Organisation for Economic Cooperation and Development, 'Due Diligence Guidance for Responsible Supply Chains of Minerals from Conflict-Affected and High-Risk Areas' (OECD, 2016) (*'Due Diligence for Minerals'*).

17 In particular, International Organisation for Standardization, 'ISO 26000 Guidance on Social Responsibility' (ISO 2010) (*'ISO 26000 Guidance'*); 'ISO 20400 Sustainable Procurement – Guidance' (ISO 2017) (*'ISO 20400 Guidance'*).

18 For link between United Nations Guiding Principles on Business and Human Rights and Organisation for Economic Cooperation and Development Guidelines for Multinational Enterprises, see Organisation for Economic Cooperation and Development, 'OECD Guidelines for Multinational Enterprises' (OECD, 2011) (*'OECD Multinational Enterprises Guidelines'*) 3–4; For link between United Nations Global Compact Principles and Organisation for Economic Cooperation and Development Guidelines for Multinational Enterprises, see UN Global Compact and the OECD, 'Guidelines for Multinational Enterprises: Complementarity and Distinctions' (2012) 2–4; For link between Organisation for Economic Cooperation and Development Guidelines for Multinational Enterprises and International Organisation for Standardization, see ISO 26000 Guidance on Social Responsibility, 'ISO 26000 and the OECD Guidelines: Practical Overview of the Linkages' (2016) (*'ISO 26000 and OECD: Practical Overview'*) 8–10; For link between Organisation for Economic Cooperation and Development Due Diligence Guidance for Responsible Supply Chains and United Nations Guiding Principles on Business and Human Rights and UN Global Compact, see *Due Diligence for Garment and Footwear Sector*, above n 16, 3, 19, and *Guidance for Agriculture*, above n 16, 16; For Link between United Nations Guiding Principles on Business and Human Rights and United Nations Global Compact, see United Nations Global Compact, 'The UN Guiding Principles on Business and Human Rights: Relationship to UN Global Compact Commitments' (Updated June 2014); For link between International Organisation for Standardization, ISO 26000 Guidance on Social Responsibility and United Nations Global Compact, see UN Global Compact and

4   *Introduction*

They apply to domestic and transnational businesses, regardless of size, sector, location or structure.[19] Although not legally enforceable, they aim to create a more responsible corporate sector.[20]

The OECD guidelines provide principles and standards of good practice for multinational companies to conduct business responsibly. They are part of the *OECD Declaration on International Investment and Multinational Enterprises* which was adopted by member-country governments in 1976 and was most recently reviewed in 2011.[21] Multinational companies operating in or from the 36 OECD countries and 12 non-OECD countries that have endorsed the declaration must follow it.[22] Although the guidelines are voluntary and not legally enforceable,[23] they are the only multilaterally-agreed and comprehensive code of responsible business conduct that governments have committed to promoting.[24] They reflect good practice for all companies, whether

---

ISO 26000, 'An Introduction to linkages between UN Global Compact Principles and ISO 26000 Core Subjects' (2010) 1; For link between International Organisation for Standardization, ISO 26000 Guidance on Social Responsibility and United Nations Guiding Principles on Business and Human Rights: see *ISO 26000 Social Responsibility* (Learn2improve) <http://www.learn2improve.nl/about-iso-26000/un-human-rights-and-iso-26000/>.

19   *ISO 26000 Guidance*, above n 17, 1; *ISO 20400 Guidance*, above n 17, vi; United Nations Office of the High Commissioner, 'Guiding Principles on Business and Human Rights' (OHCHR, 2011) ('*Guiding Principles*') 1; *OECD Multinational Enterprises Guidelines*, above n 18, 18; International Labour Organisation, 'Tripartite Declaration of Principles concerning Multinational Enterprises and Social Policy' (Report, 5th ed., 2017) ('*Tripartite Declaration*') [6].

20   *ISO 20400 Guidance*, above n 17, vi; *Guiding Principles*, above n 19, 1; *OECD Multinational Enterprises Guidelines*, above n 18, 3, 13, 17; United Nations Office of the High Commissioner, 'The Corporate Responsibility to Respect Human Rights, An Interpretative Guide' (OHCHR, 2012) ('*Interpretive Guide on Corporate Responsibility*') 1; *Guidance for Agriculture*, above n 16, 3; *Due Diligence for Garment and Footwear Sector*, above n 16, 3–4; *Due Diligence for Minerals*, above n 16, 16; *Tripartite Declaration*, above n 19 [7]; *Frequently Asked Questions, Is the UNGC legally binding?*, United Nations Global Compact <https://www.unglobalcompact.org/about/faq>.

21   Organisation for Economic Cooperation and Development, *Text of the OECD Declaration on International Investment and Multinational Enterprises* (25 May 2011) <http://www.oecd.org/investment/investment-policy/oecddeclarationoninternationalinvestmentandmultinationalenterprises.htm?>.

22   Organisation for Economic Cooperation and Development, *Declaration and Decisions on International Investment and Multinational Enterprises* <http://www.oecd.org/daf/inv/investment-policy/oecddeclarationanddecisions.htm>.

23   *OECD Multinational Enterprises Guidelines*, above n 18, 3, 13, 17.

24   Ibid 3.

multinational or domestic,[25] parent companies or local operations,[26] and are consistent with relevant laws and internationally-recognised standards.

The OECD guidelines do not override domestic laws and regulations. Governments have the right to set conditions for multinational companies to operate in their area, subject to international law. Businesses must follow domestic laws wherever they operate.[27] Although the OECD guidelines are occasionally broader in scope than local laws,[28] they are not meant to create situations where companies face conflicting requirements. Where there is conflict, businesses should try to fulfil the guidelines as closely as possible without breaking local laws.[29]

The UN Guiding Principles on Business and Human Rights provide a blueprint for States and businesses to prevent and address human rights abuses linked to business operations.[30] They are a global standard of practice that applies to all States and businesses, regardless of their size, sector, location, ownership and structure. They were developed by UN Secretary-General Special Representative on Business and Human Rights, John Ruggie,[31] and endorsed by the UN Human Rights Council in 2011.[32]

The principles recognise that companies must respect human rights, comply with all applicable laws, and provide appropriate and effective remedies to people affected by business-related human rights abuses.[33] They are not legally-binding[34] and don't create any new responsibilities under international law. But if they are to achieve real results for affected people and communities, they need to be read and understood as a whole.[35]

---

25 Ibid 18.
26 Ibid 17.
27 Ibid.
28 Ibid; *Due Diligence for Garment and Footwear Sector*, above n 16, 19.
29 *OECD Multinational Enterprises Guidelines*, above n 18, 17; *Due Diligence for Garment and Footwear Sector*, above n 16, 19–20.
30 *Interpretive Guide on Corporate Responsibility*, above n 20, 2.
31 Ibid 1.
32 Human Rights Council, *Human Rights and Transnational Corporations and Other Business Enterprises*, 17th sess, Agenda Item 3, UN Doc A/HRC/RES/17/4 (6 July 2011).
33 *Interpretive Guide on Corporate Responsibility*, above n 20, 1.
34 Ibid.
35 *Guiding Principles*, above n 19, 1.

6 *Introduction*

The UN Global Compact is a non-legally-binding framework[36] that supports participating companies to do business responsibly and sustainably. It was announced by UN Secretary-General Kofi Annan at the World Economic Forum in 1999[37] and is supported by the United Nations General Assembly.[38] Participating businesses align their strategies and operations with ten principles that cover human rights, labour, the environment and anti-corruption. They are also encouraged to help tackle society's broader challenges, such as ending extreme poverty, fighting inequality and protecting the planet, through collaboration and new ideas.[39]

The principles that are relevant to modern slavery are that businesses should: respect international human rights (Principle 1); make sure they aren't complicit in human rights abuses (Principle 2); and eliminate forced and child labour (Principles 4 and 5). Each year, participants must publish a report on their progress to implement the ten principles.

The International Organization for Standardization is a network of national standards authorities from more than 160 countries[40] which was founded in 1947.[41] International standards are developed in a lengthy process of consultation and consensus involving experts, national delegations and stakeholders from all over the world.[42]

The ISO has published more than 21,000 international standards, covering all aspects of technology and business.[43] The two standards of particular relevance to modern slavery are ISO 26000 (Social Responsibility) and ISO 20400 (Sustainable Procurement). These two standards guide all types of organisations,[44] encouraging them to go beyond what they are required to do by law. They promote a com-

---

36 *About the UN Global Compact*, United Nations Global Compact <https://www.unglobalcompact.org/about>; *Frequently Asked Questions, Is the UNGC Legally Binding?*, United Nations Global Compact <https://www.unglobalcompact.org/about/faq>.
37 Kofi Annan, 'Secretary-General Proposes Global Compact on Human Rights, Labour, Environment, in Address to World Economic Forum in Davos' (SG/SM/6881, 1 February 1999).
38 *Government Recognition*, United Nations Global Compact <https://www.unglobalcompact.org/about/government-recognition>.
39 *Our Mission*, United Nations Global Compact <https://www.unglobalcompact.org/what-is-gc/mission>.
40 *ISO 26000 and OECD: Practical Overview*, above n 18, 3.
41 Ibid.
42 Ibid.
43 Ibid.
44 *ISO 26000 Guidance*, above n 17, 1; *ISO 20400 Guidance*, above n 17, vi.

mon understanding of social responsibility and intend to complement existing initiatives in this area. The standards are neither meant to provide a basis for legal actions, complaints, defences or other claims, nor to be used as proof of how customary international law has evolved.[45]

The Tripartite Declaration of Principles Concerning Multinational Enterprises and Social Policy ('*the Declaration*') guides multinational companies, governments, and employers' and workers' organisations on good practices to follow to achieve 'decent work for all'. It covers areas such as employment, workplace relations, training, and working and living conditions.

The International Labor Organization first adopted the Declaration in 1977. It has since been amended three times, most recently in 2017.[46] Following the Declaration is voluntary and does not change responsibilities that come from ratifying any ILO conventions.[47]

The Declaration is based on principles contained in international labour standards, including the fundamental principles and rights at work, and includes guidelines on forced and child labour and remedy for human rights abuses. It states that multinational and national companies should immediately take steps to get rid of and ban forced labour in their operations[48] to comply with the minimum working age and to urgently eliminate and prohibit the worst forms of child labour.[49]

Multinational companies should also use their influence to urge their business partners to provide effective remediation for human rights abuses.[50] This includes both multinational and national businesses respecting their workers' rights to lodge complaints without any prejudice and to have them properly investigated in a formal process.[51]

As the world has become more conscious of the prevalence of modern slavery in almost every industry, whether domestic or international, consumers, investors, NGOs and policymakers have demanded greater accountability and transparency by businesses.[52]

---

45 *ISO 26000 Guidance*, above n 17, 1.
46 *Tripartite Declaration*, above n 19, 1.
47 Ibid 3 [7].
48 Ibid 8 [25].
49 Ibid [27].
50 Ibid 15 [65].
51 Ibid [66].
52 Genevieve LeBaron and Andres Rühmkorf, 'The Domestic Politics of Corporate Accountability Legislation: Struggles Over the 2015 UK Modern Slavery Act' (2017) *Socio-Economic Review* 1, 2.

8   Introduction

The development of reporting requirements is a response to a growing demand by consumers to know where and how their goods are made. Of particular focus has been businesses with supply chains that feed 'high-end consumer markets in advanced capitalist countries'.[53]

Reporting requirements require large businesses to publically provide detailed reports on their operations and global supply chains, enabling 'the court of public opinion' to rank how entities respond to modern slavery. Ultimately, this process is to allow investors and consumers to 'lead with their wallets'.[54] The four main aims of such reporting laws are: to require organisations to consider their social impact and operations; enable mass transparency and create a level playing field; encourage businesses to carefully consider their brand image and reputation; and leverage the consumers' influence to demand slavery-free goods.[55]

One of the first statutes[56] for reporting requirements was the *Californian Transparency in Supply Chains Act 2010*, which was inserted into the *Civil Code of California* and entered into force in January 2012. Modelled off the California legislation, the United Kingdom followed suit in March 2015 by introducing the *Modern Slavery Act 2015* (UK) with the Government proclaiming that it 'wants to encourage businesses to do more, not just because they are legally obliged to, but also because they recognise it is the right thing to do'.[57] The reporting requirement commenced on 29 October 2015.

---

53   Ibid 5.
54   *Harnessing Power of Business*, above n 1, 2.
55   Ibid 18.
56   This book does not address the *Corporate Duty of Vigilance Law* (France) as this book only considers modern slavery reporting requirements. The French law is broader in scope than modern slavery. The law extends to human rights and fundamental freedoms, risks and serious harm to health, safety and the environment. This book also does not address the Dutch *Child Labor Due Diligence Act*. This Act was approved on 14 May 2019; however, it is not expected to become effective until 2022 as the Government requires time to prepare a General Administrative Order to give detail to the provisions of the Act. Any analysis without the General Administrative Order would be superficial. Further, the *Modern Slavery Act* (NSW) is also not within the scope of this book. This Act was scheduled to commence operation on 1 July 2019. However, on 19 June 2019, the Act was referred to the NSW Standing Committee on Social Issues to determine (amongst other matters) whether the Commonwealth's Modern Slavery Act renders part or possibly all of the NSW Act unnecessary. This includes the Act's modern slavery reporting requirement.
57   *Transparency in Supply Chains etc. A Practical Guide* (Home Office, London, updated 2018) 3 [1.4].

Introduction 9

In December 2018, Australia introduced the *Modern Slavery Act 2018* (Cth) with a commencement date of 1 January 2019. This is the Australian Government's response to California and the United Kingdom's reporting requirements.[58] It seeks to 'contribute to the creation of an emerging international level playing field by complementing existing disclosure legislation in jurisdictions like the UK and California'.[59]

Although one of the primary objectives of the modern slavery reporting requirements is to enable the public to compare the actions of entities in order to address modern slavery, there are inconsistencies in the reporting requirements required by California, the United Kingdom and Australia.

This book first covers the drafting history of modern slavery reporting requirements in California, the United Kingdom and Australia, comprehensively detailing the parliamentary process in each jurisdiction, canvassing committee inquiries and government responses, parliamentary debates, moved amendments, final stages, and where relevant, post-enactment developments.

Following this, this book provides a comparative analysis of the modern slavery reporting requirements in California, the United Kingdom and Australia, detailing similarities and areas of divergence.

---

58 Attorney-General's Department (Cth), *Public Consultation Paper and Regulatory Impact Statement for a Modern Slavery in Supply Chains Reporting Requirement* (16 August 2017) 8.
59 Explanatory Memorandum, Modern Slavery Bill 2018 (Cth) 45.

2 The origins of the disclosure approach

California Transparency in Supply Chains Act 2010

2.1 Introduction

The *California Transparency in Supply Chains Act 2010* was the first statute of its type – a single legislative enactment dedicated to the eradication of forced labour in the operations of large businesses, and it has been the inspiration for supply chain transparency legislation in other jurisdictions.

The supply chain transparency and reporting requirements take their place within the *California Civil Code*[1] and the *California Revenue and Taxation Code*.[2] This chapter focuses on the legislative history of this short but seminally important Act, from its first tabling through to its approval and signing by Governor Arnold Schwarzenegger in September 2010.

2.2 The Bill's first iteration: SB 1649 (2008)

2.2.1 The Bill as introduced

On 22 February 2008, in the 2007–8 legislative session, Democrat Senator Steinberg, as co-sponsor of the first attempt at supply chain legislation, introduced his first version of this law passed and added to the state's statutory Codes.[3] This first Bill, although ultimately

---

1 *Civil Code 1872* (California) § 1714.43 ('*Civil Code*').
2 *Revenue and Taxation Code* 1939 (California) § 19547.5 ('*Revenue and Taxation Code*'). In SB 657 as introduced, amendments in s 3 would add a new Chapter 4.5 (commencing with Section 8305) in Division 1 of Title 2 of the *Government Code 1943* ('*Government Code*'). This section, establishing an independent Commission, was abandoned.
3 The Secretary of State 'chapters' a Bill once it has passed both houses and has been signed by the Governor (or become law without signature). All Bills that become law are given a sequential chapter number, cited by chapter and year, or referred to

Origins of the disclosure approach 11

unsuccessful, was important because it established the basic framework of the reporting requirement and was the point at which an independent Commission was both proposed and rejected, thus considerably weakening the legislation.[4]

Senator Steinberg promoted the Bill in these terms:[5]

> The primary goal of this measure is to highlight the existence of slave-labor and human trafficking throughout California. The measure also creates an opportunity for California retailers and manufacturers to demonstrate leadership in eradicating slave-labor and human trafficking. Additionally, with the information required of businesses, the measure empowers consumers to reward companies that proactively work to eradicate slave-labor and human trafficking.

The Bill was supported by several organisations, notably human rights organisations and unions.[6] Businesses were apparently not inclined to take up this opportunity to 'demonstrate leadership'. However, despite their reluctance, the legislative counsel's Bill Analysis did not, initially, list any formally declared opponents of the Bill.

Nevertheless, the Bill Analysis noted the findings and recommendations of an October 2007 Task Force Report and the fact that the Bill requires:[7]

> ...the business community to pro-actively prevent forced labor by using their economic leverage to influence human rights abuse practices within their supply chain, and enhances general awareness among the citizens of the state.

---

by the Bill number they were assigned in the Assembly or the Senate. Thus, SB 657 (2009–10) is Chapter 556, Statutes of 2010.

4 In the end, in California, free market/small-government forces prevailed, and responsibility for oversight of the scheme remained with the Attorney General.
5 California, *Senate Judiciary Committee*, 30 April 2008, Bill Analysis SB 1649, 3 [1].
6 Ibid 5: supporters included California Commission on the Status of Women; California Partnership to End Domestic Violence; Catholic Charities of California; California Labor Federation; California Teamsters; CA Conference Board of the Amalgamated Transit Union; United Food & Commercial Workers Western States Council; CA Conference of Machinists; Professional and Technical Engineers, IFPTE Local 21, Engineers and Scientists of CA, IFPTE Local 20, International Longshore and Warehouse Union; American Federation of Television and Radio Artists; Strategic Committee on Public Employees, Laborers International Union.
7 Ibid 2. The California Alliance to Combat Trafficking & Slavery Task Force ('*CA ACTS Task Force*') established to evaluate the nature and extent of human trafficking in California and effective responses.

12   *Origins of the disclosure approach*

This was to be achieved by specifying, in the Bill, that:[8]

> Every retail seller and manufacturer doing business in this state shall develop, maintain, and implement a policy setting forth its efforts to comply with federal and state law regarding the eradication of slavery and human trafficking from its supply chain.

This was the core requirement in all three versions of the Bill in total (in February, April and June 2008).[9] However, later amendments made significant changes.

2.2.2 The Bill as amended in the Senate: April 2008

The Senate, where the Bill was introduced, considered it between February and May 2008. The central provision of the Bill, requiring every retail seller and manufacturer to develop and implement a policy 'setting forth its efforts to comply' with laws to eradicate slavery from its supply chain, was retained.[10] However, the Senate's amendments added the following new and significantly more demanding sentence at the end of the central clause:[11]

> The policy shall make every reasonable effort to trace components through the supply chain back to the raw materials that are used to manufacture those goods.

In addition, new recitals were added,[12] along with a revenue threshold:[13]

> This section shall not apply to a retail seller or manufacturer having less than two million dollars ($2,000,000) in annual sales.

---

8   Ibid 1: specified in s 2(a), which would add § 1714.43 to the *Civil Code*.
9   In the form as introduced on 22 February 2008; as amended by the Senate on 22 April 2008; and as amended by the Assembly on 18 June 2008.
10 That is, § 2(a).
11 California, *Senate Judiciary Committee*, 30 April 2008, Bill Analysis SB 1649, § 2(a) (amend 22 April 2008).
12 In a newly inserted § 1, with §§ 2(a) to (e). These were carried through to the legislation in its final form.
13 Ibid § 2(c).

2.2.3 The Bill as amended in the Assembly: June 2008

After its passage through the Senate on 15 May, the Bill was sent to the Assembly.[14] In the Committee on Judiciary, the Senate's earlier amendment adding the requirement to 'make every reasonable effort to trace components through the supply chain back to the raw materials that are used to manufacture those goods' was deleted.[15] In its place, the contents of the policy were spelt out:[16]

- The policy was to be posted on the retail seller's or manufacturer's website and made available in writing upon request by a consumer (s 2(b)).
- At a minimum, the policy must include both (s 2(c)):
  - 'that the company and all the suppliers in its supply chain, including the suppliers of the raw materials incorporated into the product, will comply with the laws regarding slavery and human trafficking of the country or countries in which they are doing business' (s 2(c)(1)) and
  - 'that the company will make a good faith effort to eradicate slavery and human trafficking in its existing supply chain rather than stop doing business in the area where it discovers that its supply chain is tainted by slavery or human trafficking' (s 2(c)(2)).

The revenue threshold of $2 million was retained.[17] In addition, protections for trade secrets were added,[18] along with a remedies clause:[19]

> The exclusive remedy for a violation of this section shall be an action brought by the Attorney General for injunctive relief. Nothing in this section shall limit remedies available for a violation of any other state or federal law.

---

14 Marked in the record as 'From committee with author's amendments. Read second time. Amended. Re-referred to Committee on JUD' on 18 June 2008 (reference is to the Assembly's Committee on Judiciary, its Senate counterpart is the Senate Standing Committee on Judiciary).
15 From § 2(a).
16 In the new §§ 2(b) and (c).
17 § 2(c) becoming 2(d).
18 As § 2(e).
19 As § 2(f).

14 Origins of the disclosure approach

A commencement date of 1 January 2010 was set.[20] However, the Assembly amendments included specifications for a Commission to Combat Slavery and Human Trafficking. This necessarily required amendments to the *Government Code*[21] and changed the Bill's status from the one not requiring fiscal consideration to the one requiring that additional committee consideration. At the Assembly Appropriations Committee stage, the Bill Analysis now included fiscal impact statements:[22]

1. Presumably, since enforcement by the AG is discretionary, any enforcement would be accomplished within existing resources.
2. Ongoing (non-state) costs for the commission are unknown, but given the commission's multitude of duties, the cost could be in the range of $1 million.

The Bill foundered here, in its third iteration. By then, it was also opposed by the California Manufacturers and Technology Association (CMTA), which concluded its first statement of opposition by stating 'we would welcome further discussion on this important issue', but the Bill 'as currently drafted, is premature and imposes unnecessary liability on businesses'[23] and later declared, '[a]lthough the goals of the sponsors are well intended, this legislation is too broad and does not clearly outline how businesses should comply'.[24]

The Bill had been passed (3:2) by the Senate Judiciary Committee on 29 April 2008 and on the Senate Floor on 15 May (23:15). On 24 June it passed the Assembly Judiciary Committee (7:3) on the motion '[d]o pass and be re-referred to the Committee on Appropriations'.[25] However, when the Bill stalled in the Appropriations Committee of the Assembly on 9 July 2008, it became an inactive Bill, recorded, according to legislative practice, as 'Died—Assembly—Appropriations'.[26]

---

20 As § 2(g).
21 Proposed § 3 provided that 'A new Chapter 4.5 (commencing with Section 8305) is added to Division 1 of Title 2 of the Government Code'.
22 California, *Assembly Committee on Appropriations*, 9 July 2008, Bill Analysis SB 1649, 1.
23 California, *Assembly Committee on Judiciary*, 24 June 2008, Bill Analysis SB 1649, 4.
24 California, *Assembly Committee on Appropriations*, 9 July 2008, Bill Analysis SB 1649, 2.
25 Bill Analysis SB 657, Votes, available at SB-657 Human Trafficking, California Legislative Information <https://leginfo.legislature.ca.gov/faces/billVotesClient.xhtml?bill_id=200920100SB657>.
26 Bill Analysis SB 657, Status, available at SB-657 Human Trafficking, California Legislative Information <https://leginfo.legislature.ca.gov/faces/billStatusClient.xhtml?bill_id=200920100SB657>.

2.3 The Bill's second iteration: SB 657 (2009–10)

2.3.1 Introduction of Californian Senate Bill 657[27]

On 27 February 2009, Senator Steinberg again moved the supply chain legislation, introducing Californian Senate Bill 657 as Principal Co-author along with Assembly Members John A Pérez and Saldaña Brownley.[28] The Bill was in a form very similar to the previous Bill introduced in 2008.

Again, the Bill was a mere three sections in extent, barely two pages.[29] Those who actively supported the legislation were, again, not-for-profits including unions.[30] The California Grocers Association formally opposed the Bill from the start citing inadequate resources to monitor overseas-based suppliers.[31]

Briefly stated, the Bill proposed a commencement date for compliance of 1 January 2011, and required retail sellers and manufacturers that conduct business in California and made over $2 million in gross receipts to disclose their efforts to eradicate slavery and human trafficking from their supply chains for tangible goods offered for sale. Senator Corbett brought a concurrent resolution that the Senate '[e]ncourage the Legislature, businesses and organizations to bring visibility and support to efforts to recognize and combat human trafficking and slavery'.[32]

---

27 On the searchable database this version of the supply chain legislation is SB 657 Human trafficking (2009–10). Legislative movements and analyses on SB 657 area reached from the Bill page. Bill Analyses are available at <https://leginfo.legislature.ca.gov/faces/billAnalysisClient.xhtml?bill_id=200920100SB657#>.
28 Perez in turn had House of Assembly co-authoring partners, Assembly Members Brownley and Saldana: California, *Legislative Counsel's Digest* (27 February 2009) SB 657, as introduced (Steinberg).
29 California, *Legislative Counsel's Digest* (27 February 2009) SB 657: 'an act to add Section 1714.43 to the Civil Code, and to add Chapter 4.5 (commencing with Section 8305) to Division 1 of Title 2 of the Government Code, relating to human trafficking'.
30 California, *Assembly Committee on Judiciary*, 24 June 2008, Bill Analysis SB 1649, 5: the Coalition to Abolish Slavery & Trafficking (CAST); the California Teamsters Public Affairs Council; the California Labor Federation, the American Federation of Labor and Congress of Industrial Organizations (AFL-CIO); and Planned Parenthood Affiliates of California.
31 California, *Senate Judiciary Committee*, 21 April 2009, Bill Analysis SB 1649, 5.
32 California, *Legislative Counsel's Digest* (17 August 2010) Senate Concurrent Resolution No. 76, SCR 76, Ch 81: filed with Secretary of State and chaptered.

16 *Origins of the disclosure approach*

The first section, in the nature of recitals,[33] found and determined:

- that slavery and human trafficking 'are crimes under state, federal, and international law' (s 1(a)).[34]
- that slavery and human trafficking were universal (globally, in the US and at Californian state level)[35] and that 'consumers and businesses are often inadvertently touched by this crime through the unknowing purchase of goods that have been infected in the supply chain' (s 1(b)).[36]
- that such crimes are, because of their criminal nature, 'often hidden from view' and 'difficult to uncover and track' (s 1(c)).[37]
- that eradication of these crimes from Californian consumer goods 'will serve the ultimate goal of eradicating slavery and human trafficking worldwide' (s 1(d)).[38]
- that where this criminally exploitive conduct is found, 'a policy of engagement by business, government, and nongovernmental organizations, rather than boycotts or disengagement, is often a more successful strategy in the fight to eradicate [them]' (s 1(e)).[39]
- that Californian policy is to 'assist businesses to identify and work to eliminate' these offences from their supply chains, to educate consumers on purchasing from 'companies that responsibly manage their supply chains, and, thereby, to improve the lives of victims of slavery and human trafficking' (s 1(f)).[40]

Sections 2 and 3 as introduced added to the *Civil Code* and the *Government Code*, respectively.[41] Proposed Section 2, in brief, provided:

- 'Every retail seller and manufacturer doing business in this state shall develop, maintain, and implement a policy setting forth its

---

33 Unlike substantive provisions, the statutory statements of intent and purpose in proposed § 1 of the *California Transparency Act* do not become embedded in the California Codes that constitute the general statutory law.
34 Retained unaltered in chaptered § 2(a).
35 The first part of the statement was retained unaltered in chaptered § 2(b).
36 The second part of the statement was retained in similar terms in in the chaptered version, as part of an expanded group of recitals (in chaptered § 2(h)).
37 Retained unaltered in chaptered § 2(c).
38 Not present in the chaptered version.
39 Not present in the chaptered version.
40 While the core of this statement was retained, it underwent a change of emphasis from assisting business to ensuring the publication of information, as discussed further below.
41 It proposed to add § 2 to the *Civil Code* as Section 1714.43 and add § 3 to Division 1 of Title 2 of the *Government Code* as Chapter 4.5, commencing with § 8305.

efforts to comply with federal and state law regarding the eradication of slavery and human trafficking from its supply chain' (s 2(a)).
- Policies were to be published on the company's website and made available in writing upon a consumer's request (Section 2(b)).
- At a minimum, policies had to include both:
  - a declaration of commitment to compliance[42] (Section 2(c)(1)).
  - a declaration of commitment to eradication of the problem rather than retreat from it[43] (s 2(c)(2)).
- The Act took effect on a business only if its annual sales reached $2,000,000 (s 2(d)).
- Trade secrets were safe from disclosure (s 2(e)).
- Injunctions obtained by the Attorney General were the only form of relief from violations (s 2(f)).[44]
- The provisions of this section took effect on 1 January 2011 (s 2(g)).

Proposed Section 3, in brief, provided:

- A Commission to Combat Slavery and Human Trafficking (s 3(a)), established as a not-for-profit (s 3(e)), with a membership of nine from prescribed stakeholders (s 3(b)), funded from private sources and able to charge fees to companies who use its services and accept 'grants, donations, or funding from any source' (s 3(d)).
- The Commission would have the following powers and duties (s 3(c)):
  - Complaint investigation;
  - Policy compliance with the *Civil Code* provisions;[45]
  - Establishing educational and training programs and best practices to assist companies required to comply (helping them develop policies to combat slavery and human trafficking);
  - Reviewing company policies and certifying that they comply with best practices;

---

42 'That the company and all the suppliers in its supply chain, including the suppliers of the raw materials incorporated into the product, will comply with the laws regarding slavery and human trafficking of the country or countries in which they are doing business' (§ 2(c)(1)).
43 'That the company will make a good faith effort to eradicate slavery and human trafficking in its existing supply chain rather than only stop doing business in the area where it discovers that its supply chain is tainted by slavery or human trafficking' (§ 2(c)(2)).
44 Subject to a saving provision 'Nothing in this section shall limit remedies available for a violation of any other state or federal law'.
45 That is, the proposed new § 1714.43 of the *Civil Code*.

- Awarding exceptional efforts in combating modern slavery in their supply chains; and
- Reporting annually to the Governor and Legislature and making recommendations.

2.3.2 Senate amendments

In the first round of Senate deliberations, from March to the end of May 2009, the Bill was introduced, sent to the Committee on Rules for assignment, sent to print and returned, to be acted upon after 30 March 2009. The Bill was read a first time on 2 March 2009 and then proceeded to its assigned committee, the Committee on Judiciary, on 19 March 2009. Its hearing date there was 21 April. The Committee on Judiciary voted (3:2) to pass the legislation; however, having fiscal implications, the Bill was re-referred to the Committee on Appropriations. There, it was set for a process hearing on 22 May, with the first substantive hearing on 28 May 2009.

On 1 June 2009, the Bill emerged from the Committee on Appropriations with author amendments. This second version of the Bill, as amended by the Senate, is discussed below.

2.3.3 The Bill as amended by the Senate: 1 June 2009

Optimistically, as introduced, the Bill had included the Chapter 4.5 addition to the *Government Code* of a Commission to Combat Slavery and Human Trafficking, which meant it must pass fiscal committee scrutiny. On 1 June 2009, the Senate amended the Bill to abandon this section,[46] thus converting the Bill to a non-fiscal measure that did not require the extra level of scrutiny and approval. This was the only amendment made.

Since the Bill as amended by the Senate on 1 June 2009 had been shorn of the proposal for a Commission to Combat Slavery and Human Trafficking, there was no longer any need for insertions in the *Government Code*, or for examination for fiscal impact by a fiscal committee. The Bill was therefore withdrawn from the Senate Committee on Appropriations (on 4 January 2010) and placed on the Second Reading file. It was duly read a second time (on 5 January) and proceeded to its Third Reading in the Senate (on 28 January), where it passed the Senate with a vote of 24:13, and was then sent to the Assembly for its consideration.[47]

---

46 Proposed § 3.
47 *California Transparency in Supply Chains Act of 2010* (2009) Bill Text CA SB 657, Version 01 June 2009, amended in the Senate.

2.4 Assembly amendments

The Bill had a more erratic passage through the Assembly. On 28 January 2010, the Bill was read for the first time in the Assembly, and then sent to the Committee on Judiciary on 18 February 2010. There, with author amendments, it was read a second time, amended again, and re-referred to the Committee on Judiciary for consideration on 23 June 2010. This version, in which the most significant amendments were made, is discussed in the following subsections.

2.4.1 The Bill as amended by the Assembly: 23 June 2010

For the first time, SB 657 was given its title, the *California Transparency in Supply Chains Act of 2010*. The proposed commencement date was extended from 1 January 2011 to 1 January 2012.[48] Rather than developing, maintaining and implementing 'policies related to their compliance with federal and state law regarding the eradication of slavery and human trafficking', retailers and manufacturers were now required to 'disclose their efforts to eradicate' it 'from their supply chains', and the threshold revenue was increased from $2 million to $100 million in gross receipts. A 'specified statement of legislative intent regarding slavery and human trafficking' was also included.[49]

Section 2 now set out the recitals carried over from previous versions of the Bill,[50] with some changes:

- The 'ultimate goal of eradicating slavery and human trafficking worldwide' was cut, along with the assertion that 'a policy of engagement by business, government, and non-governmental organizations, rather than boycotts or disengagement, is often a more successful strategy in the fight to eradicate this criminally exploitive conduct'.
- Legislative and government efforts were recorded (s 2(d)–(g)), but it was noted that market-directed efforts had been lacking and that the market was 'a key impetus for these crimes' (s 2(f)). The US Department of Labor had, in 2009, 'named 122 goods from

---

48 *California Transparency in Supply Chains Act of 2010* (2009) Bill Text CA SB 657, amended in the Assembly, § 3(e).
49 *California Transparency in Supply Chains Act of 2010* (2009) Bill Text CA SB 657, amended in the Assembly.
50 As summarised at 2.3.1 above, comparing the first, introduced version with the final version as chaptered. All these changes were made at this stage, in the Bill as amended on 23 June 2010.

58 countries that are believed to be produced by forced labour or child labour in violation of international standards' (s 2(g)), and that (as in previous versions) '[c]onsumers and businesses are inadvertently promoting and sanctioning these crimes through the purchase of goods and products that have been tainted in the supply chain' (s 2 (h)). Without public disclosures, consumers were 'at a disadvantage in being able to distinguish companies on the merits of their efforts to supply products free from the taint of slavery and trafficking' or 'force the eradication of slavery and trafficking by way of their purchasing decisions' (s 2(i)).

- The policy of the state was no longer to 'assist California businesses to identify and work to eliminate'[51] slavery and human trafficking; it was now to *'ensure large retailers and manufacturers provide consumers with information regarding their efforts to eradicate'* slavery and human trafficking 'from their supply chains, to educate consumers on how to purchase goods produced by companies that responsibly manage their supply chains, and, thereby, to improve the lives of victims of slavery and human trafficking' (s 2(j)).[52]

The central provision, the addition of a positive duty to the *Civil Code*, was now a heavily amended Section 3. These significant changes were:

- The threshold amount was now $100 million (s 3(a)).
- Rather than being required to 'develop, maintain, and implement a policy setting forth its efforts to comply with federal and state law regarding the eradication of' slavery and human trafficking, a company was now required to 'disclose its efforts to eradicate' them from its supply chain (s 3(a)).[53]
- The change in emphasis from *policy* to *disclosure* was key: the thrust of the Act was now to regulate what was to be disclosed rather than what was to be done, and the remainder of the requirements flowed from this change.
- The disclosure in s 3(a) was, as before, to be posted on the website, but an alternative path of disclosure was added: 'in the event the retail seller or manufacturer does not have an Internet Web site, consumers shall be provided the written disclosure within 30 days of receiving a written request for the disclosure from a consumer' (s 3 (b)).

---

51 The wording in previous subsection (f).
52 In the second part of this subsection, only the words italicised were new.
53 § 3(a) goes on to state that for the purposes of this section, 'doing business in this state' has the same meaning as in § 23101 of the *Revenue and Taxation Code*.

Origins of the disclosure approach 21

- In place of a policy to comply with laws and make good faith attempts to eradicate slavery and human trafficking rather than 'only stop doing business in the area', a company was now required (s 3(c)) to 'disclose to what extent the retail seller or manufacturer does each of the following':[54]

  1 Engages in third-party verification of product supply chains to evaluate and address risks of human trafficking and slavery.
  2 Conducts independent, unannounced audits of suppliers to evaluate supplier compliance with company standards for trafficking and slavery in supply chains.
  3 Requires suppliers to certify that raw materials incorporated into the product comply with the laws regarding slavery and human trafficking of the country or countries in which they are doing business.
  4 Maintains internal accountability standards and procedures for employees or contractors failing to meet company standards regarding slavery and trafficking.
  5 Provides company employees and management training on human trafficking and slavery, particularly with respect to mitigating risks within the supply chains of products.

Injunctive relief by the Attorney General remained unchanged as the exclusive remedy for a violation (s 3(d)).[55]

2.4.2 The Bill as amended by the Assembly: 30 June 2010

Assembly Member Saldaña Brownley was now the named co-author of the Bill.[56] Two substantive changes were made in this version, in line with the previous shift from policy to disclosure, but further eroding any positive duty:

- The mandated degree of effort was changed by deleting the requirement to *'develop, maintain, and* disclose' efforts to eradicate modern slavery from supply chains, leaving the requirement as merely to *'disclose*, as set forth in subdivision (c)' (s 3(a), emphasis added).

---

54 Each of these §§ (1) to (5) is new in this version of the Bill.
55 With a standard disclaimer that 'Nothing in this section shall limit remedies available for a violation of any other state or federal law': § 3(d).
56 *California Transparency in Supply Chains Act of 2010* Bill Text CA SB 657, Version 30 June 2010, amended in the Assembly.

- However, in what was clearly a compromise, failure to do anything now had to be acknowledged: 'the company must disclose ... its efforts ... including the absence of any such efforts' (s 3(a)).[57]

In addition, the website requirement was expanded to require 'a conspicuous and easily understood link to the required information placed on the business' homepage' (s 3(b)).

The rationale for these changes is set out in the Bill Analysis prepared for the hearing on 29 June, which gave the backdrop to the legislation, including more information about the current and increasing prevalence of offences. Quoting the Bill's author in describing the measure as 'A Natural Place To Redouble Our Efforts', the Analysis concluded:[58]

> California consumers and businesses appear to be uniquely positioned to drive human rights violations out of the supply chains of products sold within California borders by virtue of their ability to translate the values pronounced by the U.S. Department of Labor into demonstrable impact by virtue of their choice and simple purchasing power.

The Analysis also noted that the measure's increased threshold was 'prudent':[59]

> While this exemption naturally does not alleviate small businesses from actually complying with federal and state law on human trafficking, it appropriately recognizes that they may not have the same type of ability or resources to exert economic influence on their suppliers as do the state's largest businesses.

2.4.2.1 Supporters of the measure

The Bill Analysis cites, as an example 'reflective of the many letters of support for the bill',[60] the co-sponsor Consumer Federation of

---

57 Consequential changes appeared in § 3(c)), which also had some changes in numbering of §§ from (1), (2), etc. to (A), (B), etc. The new § 3(c)(1) required disclosure 'to what extent, *if any*,' effort was made, and a new § 3(c)(2) provided: 'The disclosure described in subdivision (a) shall include the absence or lack of any efforts by the retail seller or manufacturer as to each of the actions specified in paragraph (1)'.
58 California, *Assembly Committee on Judiciary*, 29 June 2010, Bill Analysis SB 657, 9.
59 Ibid.
60 Ibid 11: the registered supporters at this stage were Alliance to Stop Slavery and End Trafficking (co-sponsor); Coalition to Abolish Slavery & Trafficking (co-sponsor);

Origins of the disclosure approach 23

California's submission that consumers needed to be able to 'purchase products without fear of inadvertently supporting human trafficking' and required critical information about the efforts of business in order to 'make the most informed purchasing decisions possible'.[61]

Others described the measure as 'a crucial step in reducing the demand for slave-made products by providing a tool for consumers, including businesses, to be better informed' and enabling concerned consumers to 'compare company efforts' in their supply chains. The requirements were 'simple' and 'basic', yet would help provide the transparency needed to support informed choice. They also argued that transparency would 'benefit companies that are struggling to do the right thing while competing against companies that are unfairly and illegally using slave labor'.[62]

2.4.2.2 Opponents of the measure

At this stage, the registered opposition to the measure had grown substantially, beyond the original Grocers Association, to include chambers of commerce and technology interests.[63] In a joint letter of opposition, they argued two main points, to which the Analysis responds in a tone that suggests rebuke:[64]

- *First*, that the measure 'would require companies to develop policies with regard to [sic] its entire supply chain, which can include entities far outside the borders of California or the United States. The policies would need to address specific issues such as third-party verification of product supply chain, independent unannounced audits and certification of raw materials'.
- In response, the Analysis notes that the measure 'does not in fact require companies to develop any policies at all', spells out the threshold provision, and notes that 'less than 5% of the state's

---

Consumer Federation of California (co-sponsor); Alliance to End Slavery and Trafficking; California Catholic Conference; California Commission on the Status of Women; California Labor Federation, AFL-CIO; California School Employees Association; California Teamsters Public Affairs Council; Free the Slaves; Los Angeles District Attorney's Office; Not For Sale; Planned Parenthood Affiliates of California; Polaris Project.

61 Ibid 11.
62 Ibid 12.
63 Ibid 12: California Chamber of Commerce; California Grocers Association; California Manufacturers and Technology Association; California Retailers Association; Corona Chamber of Commerce; TechAmerica.
64 Ibid 12.

24 *Origins of the disclosure approach*

businesses need disclose their efforts, whatever they may be' including doing nothing.
- *Second*, that it was wrong in principle to use private businesses 'as the enforcement arm for federal and state laws' since federal and state government entities were responsible for those laws.
- In response, the Analysis noted that the measure did not require 'the relative narrow number of designated large companies to do anything other than post specified information on their websites and also make such information available to interested consumers'. There was no requirement 'to act as an enforcement arm of government; indeed, the bill acknowledges that these businesses are still completely free to do anything they want about their efforts to fight human trafficking and slavery, they simply need to note this information on their websites and make such information available to interested consumers'.
- *In addition*, they argued that 'the practical effect ... will be to hold certain companies up for ridicule and condemnation for "failing" to address issues they are powerless to address'.
- In response, the Analysis again noted the narrow scope of the measure: a small number of large companies who only had to 'post specified information on their web sites and also make such information available to interested consumers' and that '[i]f the information the business provides is found by some consumers to reflect inadequate attention to this issue, then that is a business choice as to whether that is a wise course of action'. Further, '[a]s to whether businesses here in California are completely powerless to address the issue, 'there is ample evidence' to the contrary: citing the CA ACTS Task Force, the analysis notes that 'some respected California businesses ... have already taken the lead to adopt their own codes of conduct ... for their suppliers and sub-contractors, voluntarily using their substantial economic power to influence labor and human rights practices within their supply chains'.

2.4.2.3 *Clarifications*

In light of the objections, the Bill Analysis set out suggested clarifying amendments:[65]

> In order to maximize clarity in the bill that the measure does not require the specified large business entities to do anything regarding human trafficking and slavery within their product supply

---

65 Ibid 13.

chains, other than disclose what if anything they are doing, including nothing, the Committee may wish to explore with the author the possible merits of the following minor clarifications to the Section 3 of the bill.

These were the amendments, discussed above, to state the extent 'if any' to which an effort had been made; including the 'absence or lack of any efforts', and to make the website link 'conspicuous and easily understood' and on the home page.

On 29 June 2010, the Bill proceeded in the Committee on Judiciary, which voted to pass it as amended (7:2). This version, which proceeded to Second Reading in the Assembly on 30 June, is discussed in the following section.

2.5 The Act in final form

2.5.1 *The Bill as amended by the Assembly: 20 August 2010*

On 1 July 2010, the amended Bill was read a second time and proceeded to a Third Reading on 20 August 2010, where it entered a last round of amendments and Third Readings on 23 August (passed 49 votes to 27)[66] and 26 August (passed 44 votes to 24),[67] and was put to the vote. This was the last point at which the Bill was changed – from here on, it had the form of the chaptered version that passed into law as the *California Transparency in Supply Chains Act 2010*.

At this stage, the Bill was again made subject to fiscal committee review, as it had been in the versions that proposed a Commission. However, while the establishment of a Commission would have necessitated amendment of the *Government Code*, the changes made in August 2010 required changes to the *Revenue and Taxation Code* as a result of the insertion of a new Section 4, which imposed duties on the Franchise Tax Board.

The changes made by the amendments linked the measure to definitions in the *Revenue and Taxation Code*, with consequent changes of numbering within sections:

- Disclosure by companies (with a threshold now clarified as having annual *worldwide* gross receipts) was now limited to 'efforts to

[66] Bill Analysis SB 657, History available at SB-657 Human Trafficking, California Legislative Information <https://leginfo.legislature.ca.gov/faces/billHistoryClient.xhtml?bill_id=200920100SB657>.
[67] Ibid.

26 *Origins of the disclosure approach*

eradicate slavery and human trafficking from their *direct* supply chains (thus severely restricting the scope of disclosure)[68] for *tangible goods offered for sale*' (s 3(1)),[69] thus eliminating any doubt about intellectual property (a concern of technology companies that opposed the Bill).
- The framework of disclosure of risk in the form of Verification, Audit, Certification, Internal accountability and Training (VACIT) introduced in June[70] was amended so that the disclosure must specify:
  - if verification was not conducted by a third party (s 3(C)(1))
  - if verification was not an independent, unannounced audit (s 3(C)(2)).
- Disclosure of requirements placed on suppliers was limited to direct suppliers (s 3(C)(3))[71]
- Disclosure of staff training was required only for 'who have direct responsibility for supply chain management' (s 3(C)(5)).
- The requirement to disclose a lack of effort, introduced in the previous round of amendments, was deleted.[72]
- The disclosure requirements were further amended by adding definitions of the terms 'doing business in this state', 'gross receipts', 'manufacturer', and 'retail seller', each defined according to the *Revenue and Taxation Code* (s 3(2)(A), (B), (C) and (D)).[73]
- The Franchise Tax Board was now required to provide the Attorney General with a list of retail sellers and manufacturers that were subject to the measure, based on tax returns filed for taxable years beginning on or after 1 January 2011 and including the entity's name and Californian identification number.[74]

---

68 Contrary to the CA ACTS Task Force recommendation, 'within' their supply chain: cf *the CA ACTS Final Report*, above n 7.
69 Adding § 1714.43(a)(1) to the *Civil Code*.
70 As summarised above.
71 This section previously referred to suppliers of 'raw' materials; 'raw' was now deleted.
72 From previous § 3(2).
73 Respectively §§ 23101, 25120, § 18401ff and again, § 18401ff of Part 10.2 of Division 2 of the *Revenue and Taxation Code*.
74 Adding § 19547.5(a)(1) to the *Revenue and Taxation Code*.

2.5.2 Changes between the introduced and enrolled versions

As the above discussion shows, the differences between SB 657 as it was introduced in February 2009 and the final, chaptered version signed into law by the Governor on 30 September 2010 are changes of substance as well as emphasis.

A new Section 1 states that '[t]his act shall be known, and may be cited, as the California Transparency in Supply Chains Act of 2010', thus forcing a change of number for proposed Section 1, which now becomes Section 2.

The new Section 2 largely reproduces Section 1 as introduced, but with a significant shift of emphasis from 'assisting businesses to identify and work to eliminate slavery and human trafficking from their supply chains' to 'ensure[ing] large retailers and manufacturers provide consumers with information regarding their efforts to eradicate slavery and human trafficking from their supply chains'.[75] A new subsection reinforces this change of emphasis, being framed as the need for publicly available information on which to judge corporate merit:[76]

> Absent publicly available disclosures, consumers are at a disadvantage in being able to distinguish companies on the merits of their efforts to supply products free from the taint of slavery and trafficking. Consumers are at a disadvantage in being able to force the eradication of slavery and trafficking by way of their purchasing decisions.

The new Section 2 thus offers a rather different narrative from that envisioned by the CA ACTS Task Force in 2007 and Senator Steinberg in introducing the Senate Bill. It had moved away from mutual effort and support through reciprocal roles of government (federal and state) and market players (companies, consumers and investors), with a Commission as a central authority responsible for consolidating oversight and education functions. It was now consumers, rather than governments, who would 'force the eradication of slavery and trafficking by way of their purchasing decisions'[77] and they would be given the power to do so by 'publicly available disclosures' so they could 'distinguish companies on the merits of their efforts to supply products free from the

---

75 Chaptered § 1(j).
76 Chaptered § 1(i).
77 Ibid.

taint of slavery and trafficking'.[78] Consumers would no longer be 'at a disadvantage' which could lead them to 'inadvertently [promote] and [sanction] these crimes through the purchase of goods and products that have been tainted in the supply chain'.[79] The policy was now to ensure that large retailers and manufacturers supplied the information that would 'educate consumers on how to purchase goods produced by companies that responsibly manage their supply chains, and, thereby, to improve the lives of victims of slavery and human trafficking'.[80]

The new recitals added to Section 1 set the scope of government responsibility by, in effect, claiming that the government had already done its bit for criminal law and victim support:

> In recent years, significant legislative efforts have been made to capture and punish the perpetrators of these crimes.[81]
>
> ...
>
> Significant legislative efforts have also been made to ensure that victims are provided with necessary protections and rights.[82]

However, it acknowledged a gap:[83]

> Legislative efforts to address the market for goods and products tainted by slavery and trafficking have been lacking, the market being a key impetus for these crimes.

The US Government had clarified the issue:[84]

> In September 2009, the United States Department of Labor released a report ... which named 122 goods from 58 countries that are believed to be produced by forced labor or child labor in violation of international standards.

---

78 Ibid.
79 Chaptered § 1(h), moved from § 1(b) of SB 657 as introduced.
80 Chaptered § 1(j).
81 Chaptered § 1(d).
82 Chaptered § 1(e).
83 Chaptered § 1(f).
84 Chaptered §s 1(g). That report was required by the *Trafficking Victims Protection Reauthorization Acts* of 2005 and 2008. The list is now published 'every other year' and in its last iteration, 30 September 2016, 'the List of Goods Produced by Child Labor or Forced Labor comprises 139 goods from 75 countries': see Bureau of International Labour Affairs, the List of Goods Produced by Child Labor or Forced Labor, United States Department of Labour <https://www.dol.gov/agencies/ilab/list-goods-produced-child-labor-or-forced-labor-0>.

In addition, the aspirational statement that eradication of these crimes from Californian consumer goods 'will serve the ultimate goal of eradicating slavery and human trafficking worldwide' had been removed,[85] along with the preferred method of action where slavery is found: 'a policy of engagement by business, government, and nongovernmental organizations, rather than boycotts or disengagement, is often a more successful strategy in the fight to eradicate [them]'.[86] Now it was up to consumers to exercise their market power.[87]

Original Section 2, the section adding Section 1714.43 to the *Civil Code*, was now Section 3, with the differences discussed above, and there was now a Section 4 which, rather than establishing a Commission, amended the *Revenue and Taxation Code* to provide some measure of oversight at government level, in the form of supplying lists about companies who appeared to fall within the legislation.

Original Section 3, the section that would have added a Commission to Combat Slavery and Human Trafficking, to the *Government Code*,[88] had been lost in the first round of amendments – a substantial weakening of the regime, since this central plank of the proposal would have vested significant power in the hands of a central organisation dedicated to complaint investigation, education and training, a review and best practice–setting role, with awards as an incentive, and a reporting function.

However, there was now a start, and a new emphasis on businesses and the transparency of their operations.

2.6 Signing the Act into law

In its compromised form, reflecting the shift of emphasis that favoured the Bill's opponents, having been passed by the Assembly on 20 August 2010, the Bill was sent back to the Senate on 26 August, where it remained as unfinished business until 30 August. On that date the Senate voted to concur in the Assembly amendments (Ayes 22, Noes 14) and sent the Bill to enrolment.[89] Enrolled on 3 September, this final version was approved by the Governor on 30 September, and on that day chaptered by the Secretary of State as Chapter 556, Statutes of 2010.[90]

---

85 § 1(d) in the original version as introduced.
86 § 1(e) in the original version as introduced.
87 Chaptered §§ 1(h),(i),(j) as discussed above.
88 Chapter 4.5 (commencing with § 8305) to be added to Division 1 of Title 2 of the *Government Code*.
89 Bill Analysis SB 657, History available at SB-657 Human Trafficking, California Legislative Information <https://leginfo.legislature.ca.gov/faces/billHistoryClient.xhtml?bill_id=200920100SB657>.
90 Ibid.

3 Modern Slavery Act UK
Transparency in supply chains provision

3.1 Introduction

The UK supply chain transparency and reporting requirement on which this chapter focuses is found in Part 6 of the *Modern Slavery Act 2015* (UK),[1] and not in a separate legislative instrument, as in California and Australia. The UK provision also goes beyond its precursor Californian legislation.[2] It broadens the scope of disclosure regimes of this type by requiring large organisations of all kinds – not just retailers and manufacturers – to issue an annual statement disclosing the steps they have taken, or not taken, to combat modern slavery offences occurring in their own operations and supply chains. This chapter traces the legislative history of the UK Act from December 2013 to a recent review of the Act in 2018 and the UK Government response in 2019, focusing on the transparency in supply chains provision.

3.2 Consultation and development phase

In March 2013, after an 18-month review, the Centre for Social Justice issued a report, *It Happens Here*, which detailed the distressing facts of modern slavery in the UK and recounted the considerable anti-slavery work of NGOs to that point.[3] In October 2013, the Home Office

---

1 *Modern Slavery Act 2015* (UK) c 30, Part 6, s 54, 'Transparency in supply Chains etc', supported by the *Modern Slavery Act 2015 (Transparency in Supply Chain) Regulations 2015*.
2 *California Transparency in Supply Chains Act 2010*, Cal Civ Code § 1714.43 ('California Transparency Act').
3 In addition, data was collected by the All-Party Parliamentary Group on Human Trafficking and Modern Day Slavery <www.humantraffickingfoundation.org/appg>.

commissioned a parliamentary committee to conduct a pre-legislative stage[4] that included evidence reviews.[5]

This was quickly followed by a draft Modern Slavery Bill[6] published by the Home Office on 16 December 2013 together with a white paper setting out the Government's non-legislative approach to modern slavery.[7]

In response to its October commission to lead a series of evidence sessions, the Modern Slavery Bill Evidence Review Panel also reported to the Home Secretary in December.[8] The Panel's work informed development of the final Bill and an action plan.[9] Although supply chain measures were a key recommendation,[10] they were then at a preliminary stage of development. The Californian legislation was noted with approval as something to 'build and improve on'.[11]

Initially, companies should be required to state in their annual reports and on their websites what concrete measures they had taken, and appoint 'a special non-executive director with the responsibility of heading their antislavery activities'. Two years should be allowed before the requirements came into effect, and the new Anti-Slavery Commissioner 'will need to review how the new statutory code of practice works, and if necessary, make recommendations to the Government

---

4 This pre-legislative stage Committee was then referred by the Government as the PLS Committee, in contradistinction to the Joint Committee discussed at 3.3 below, which is referred to as 'the Joint Committee'.
5 Commissioning Letter from the Home Secretary, Theresa May to the Frank Field, 10 October 2013 to form a Modern Slavery Bill Evidence Review Panel.
6 Prepared by the Home Office and introduced by James Brokenshire, along with reports: Home Office, *Draft Modern Slavery Bill: European Convention on Human Rights, Memorandum by the Home Office* (2013); and Home Office, *Draft Modern Slavery Bill: A Impact Assessment* (6 November 2013).
7 The white paper was published under the 2010–15 Conservative and Liberal Democrat coalition government: Home Office and Theresa May (Secretary of State for the Home Department), *Modern Slavery White Paper Published*, UK Government (16 December 2013).
8 Elizabeth Butler-Sloss, Frank Filed, John Randall, Centre for Social Justice, *Establishing Britain as a World Leader in the Fight Against Modern Slavery: Report of the Modern Slavery Bill Evidence Review* (16 December 2013) ('*Evidence Review Panel Report*'). The *Evidence Review Panel Report* was presented to the Home Secretary on 16 December 2013.
9 To be published in Spring 2014: Theresa May (Secretary of State for the Home Department), Modern Slavery: Written Statement to Parliament (Speech delivered to Parliament, London, 16 December 2013).
10 *Evidence Review Panel Report*, above n 8, 14 ('Encouraging Transparency in Supply Chains'), 21, 43–9, 52–3.
11 Ibid 6, 21.

for its reform'.[12] Initially, expansion of existing Gangmasters legislation was considered a useful approach. Further, the value 'leading by example' was stressed:[13]

> The Panel believes that the Government should set the very best example possible by first meeting the same requirements through all local and national Government procurement before requiring companies to disclose their information.

After reviewing the Californian legislation and judging it a 'good first step',[14] the Panel recommended that if possible linking to existing reporting structures. Ultimately, this proposed efficiency did not become part of the reporting regime.

3.3 The Joint Committee process

Early in the following year, a Joint House of Commons–House of Lords Committee on the Draft Modern Slavery Bill[15] was appointed to consider and report on the draft Modern Slavery Bill published in December 2013. The Joint Committee's role was to take written and oral evidence and make recommendations in a report to both Houses.

3.3.1 Call for written submissions

On 24 January 2014, the newly formed Parliamentary Joint Committee on the Draft Modern Slavery Bill sought written submissions from all interested parties, with a little over two weeks to respond to its deadline of 10 February.[16] The general nature of the invitation meant that supply chains were not specifically mentioned, so it would be understandable if affected companies were not aware that this issue would become relevant for them.

---

12 Ibid 6.
13 Ibid 14.
14 Ibid 34.
15 The Commons Members of this Committee were appointed on 9 January 2014; the Lords Members were appointed on 15th January 2014.
16 Parliamentary Joint Committee on the draft Modern Slavery Bill, *Call for Evidence: Have Your Say on the Draft Modern Slavery Bill* (24 January 2014).

Modern Slavery Act UK 33

3.3.2 Hearings taking evidence in person

On Thursday 30 January 2014, the Joint Committee called witnesses[17] whom it wished to hear in person on the definition of 'modern slavery' to be used in the Act 'so as to cover a broad range of current and future forms of exploitation, and in a way that is clear and simple to use and understand for the public, victims and the criminal justice system'.[18] The concern was, in particular, whether 'cutting and pasting' the definition of 'slavery' from the 1926 Convention would suffice, 'particularly where victims have been subjected to multiple types of exploitation'.[19] Baroness Butler-Sloss made clear that advice was being sought as a result of 'criticism by other witnesses, particularly Peter Carter ... who thinks we should bin the cross-clauses', and she was doubtful about the value of complex definitions that imported old notions of property law. From a practising barrister's perspective,[20] the areas of overlap opened up possible gaps between offences in the absence of a single broad definition, which was preferable. The Baroness was concerned about simplicity from the perspective of police, prosecutors and juries.[21]

Professor Allain, taking a different view,[22] thought the separate, traditional definition of 'slavery' should be retained; he noted that the UK took the lead in drafting the definitions in the 1926 and 1956 Conventions, and in the 1998 Rome Statute for the International Criminal Court; and that the 1926 definition had the virtue of legal certainty. He cited the Australian experience as showing that the definition is

---

17 All oral and written evidence is published on the Committee's webpages: Parliamentary Joint Committee on the draft Modern Slavery Bill, *Joint Committee on the Draft Modern Slavery Bill – Publications*, UK Parliament <https://www.parliament.uk/business/committees/committees-a-z/joint-select/draft-modern-slavery-bill/written-evidence/?type=Oral#pnlPublicationFilter>.
18 Video of the meeting (10.35am to 11.41am) is available at Draft Modern Slavery Bill Committee, *Video of Meeting* (30 January 2014) UK Parliament Live <https://www.parliamentlive.tv/Event/Index/2e492b73-6d16-4b8b-9c63-3ff04b9b655d> ('*Video of Committee Meeting 30 January 2014*').
19 Ibid: Elizabeth Butler-Sloss in the chair.
20 Ibid: Riel Karmy-Jones, Barrister, Red Lion Chambers, who also thought judges should be trained by judicial colleges and possibly also not be assigned to these cases unless they had received that training.
21 This concern was echoed in the hearings on 12 March 2014: the Act would be accessed by non-lawyers and should be readily understandable.
22 *Video of Committee Meeting 30 January 2014*, above n 18, at 11:00: Professor Jean Allain (then of School of Law, Queen's University, Belfast).

sufficiently clear to obtain prosecutions and is 'internally consistent within the law'.[23]

Seeking lessons for the UK, on 24 February the Joint Committee heard evidence from US Ambassador-at-Large, Luis CdeBaca, mainly on the US (rather than Californian) approach to tackling modern slavery.[24] The Ambassador recommended a 'three P' approach (Prosecution, Protection, Prevention, based in the Palermo Protocol, with a duty to deal with the problem locally as well as transnationally) as the only effective solution;[25] he stressed the importance of the UK law as an example for other countries, in the Commonwealth and beyond.[26]

An important observation the Ambassador made about corporate social responsibility (CSR) was that voluntary codes of practice end up in 'a different place' within corporate structures (being handled by CSR officers), whereas mandatory compliance tends to be handled by general counsel or directors, because it is part of a filing requirement. It is then in the hands of the serious heart of the corporation, and in that way, 'mandatory trumps voluntary'. Voluntary codes do help with norm-setting; however, mandatory regimes simply must be complied with.[27]

Of the Californian regime, the Ambassador remarked that some of the disclosures have been 'very interesting', demonstrating engagement and a clearly iterative process that would not have occurred in the absence of the regime, and appears not to have been driven by 'plaintiffs lawyers' (i.e., litigation claims).

Asked by Mr Field whether, given that many large UK companies already comply with the Californian legislation, the UK might just 'pick it up and put it into our Bill', the Ambassador agreed that the Californian legislation would be a good fallback position, but that he would be inclined to 'open the bidding a little bit higher' than the fallback: 'why not try for something a little better?'[28]

---

23 Citing with approval the High Court of Australia's reasoning in *The Queen v Tang* [2008] HCA 39, which clarified lingering definitional issues in the shift from human rights law to criminal law, and cleared the way for successful prosecutions.
24 As reported at Parliamentary Joint Committee on the draft Modern Slavery Bill, *Committee Hears Evidence on the US Approach to Tackling Modern Slavery* (26 February 2014). See Draft Modern Slavery Bill Committee, *Video of Meeting* (26 February 2014) UK Parliament Live <www.parliamentlive.tv/Event/Index/37f67147-58b9-46ba-af60-29cf3fed6807> ('*Video of Committee Meeting 26 February 2014*').
25 In the UK this became Four Ps: Pursue, Prevent, Protect and Prepare based on Professor Silverman's research.
26 *Video of Committee Meeting 26 February 2014*, above n 24.
27 Ibid: albeit that at that stage there had only been only 14 months of experience under the *California Transparency Act*.
28 Ibid.

On 10 March 2014, the Joint Committee heard evidence from three organisations with supply chains (Primark, Sainsbury and Tesco),[29] then considered how effective and enforceable the Bill's provisions would be, and what effect changes to legal aid and immigration law would have.[30]

At this stage, discussion on the content and form of the draft Bill was directed at consolidating and simplifying existing criminal offences relating to slavery and human trafficking and introducing civil orders to restrict the activity of those involved in or convicted of slavery and trafficking offences. The appointment of an Anti-Slavery Commissioner was included to 'encourage good practice in the prevention, detection, investigation and prosecution of offences'.

On 12 March 2014, the Joint Committee heard its final evidence,[31] from the Home Office Minister for Modern Slavery and Organised Crime, Karen Bradley, on the extent to which the Government was willing to rewrite the Bill in response to the evidence already received by the Joint Committee. The Joint Committee was concerned about the standing of the Commissioner, the danger of appointing a 'grandstander';[32] the risk that of the Commissioner being given a range of cross-governmental duties but being beholden to departmental interests, as the Committee had found to be the case in Europe; the Commissioner needed both genuine independence and 'clout' beyond prosecution power.[33] The Home Office response was that the Commissioner was envisaged as the person who would 'put the rocket up the law enforcement agencies', and that was 'where we really want the focus to be'.

The Joint Committee only briefly turned its attention to supply chain issues,[34] noting that Primark, Sainsbury and Tesco had, in their

---

29 As reported at Parliamentary Joint Committee on the draft Modern Slavery Bill, *Committee Hears Evidence from Supply Chains* (10 March 2014). Speakers include Paul Lister, Company Secretary of Associated British Foods plc (retail division Primark); Giles Bolton, Ethical Trading Director, Tesco and Judith Batchelar, Director of Brand.
30 Ibid: interviewing Caroline Young, Deputy Director, and Liam Vernon, Head of the UK Human Trafficking Centre, National Crime Agency Organised Crime Command; Sarah Rapson, Director General, UK Visas and Immigration; Zofia Duszynska, Legal Director and Shauna Gillan, Legal Officer, Immigration Law Practitioners' Association.
31 As reported at Parliamentary Joint Committee on the draft Modern Slavery Bill, *Joint Committee Hears Its Final Evidence on the Draft Modern Slavery Bill* (12 March 2014); Draft Modern Slavery Bill Committee, *Video of Meeting* (12 March 2014).
32 Ibid 14:00 min (approximately).
33 Ibid 14:30 min: questioning by Caroline Spellman.
34 Ibid 14:40 min: questioning by Andrew Stunell.

evidence, expressed no real reservations to the inclusion of something similar to the Californian provisions in the UK Act, or in changes to the *Companies Act 2006* (UK) c. 46 (*'Companies Act'*). Ms Bradley, in response, asked for further time to develop an effective approach. She noted the importance of the issue, which had been stressed by NGOs, and said that she had already asked if 'we can start having conversations with business to explore the best way to do this, because I do want to make sure we have a process and a system in place that actually tackles the problem and delivers results'.[35] Sir Andrew Stunell[36] noted that 'as ever, the good companies are doing it anyway, and the bad companies don't care', making it important to have legislative authority to wield against the 'bad' ones. While Ms Bradley agreed, she was keen to avoid 'meaningless legislation' or legislation that was burdensome to companies that are already behaving well; the Bill was only 'part of the process' and other parallel efforts were proceeding. The Home Office was meeting with Fair Trade to explore its approach, where public awareness was a central plank in the effort to improve labour conditions.

3.3.3 The Joint Committee draft Bill report

In the 2013–14 Session, the Lords and Commons jointly released the Report on the Draft Modern Slavery Bill, which included the Bill itself along with formal minutes.[37] In this phase, the Gangmasters option was considered, along with a new approach suggested by barrister Peter Carter, 'the Bribery Act model' of due diligence. However, the Joint Committee accepted evidence that this risk-based model would be 'much more burdensome than some of the other options…'.[38]

The Joint Committee noted that publicly listed companies ('quoted companies') that are required to lodge a strategic statement under companies legislation can repurpose that information for their Modern Slavery Statement. This means 'it is not necessary for an organisation to start from scratch', but statements 'should … refer to actual steps undertaken or begun'.[39]

---

35 Ibid 14:50 min (Karen Bradley).
36 Andrew Stunell was a Liberal Democrat MP. He stood down, then was made a life peer in 2015, taking his place in the House of Lords.
37 House of Lords, House of Commons Joint Committee on the Draft Modern Slavery Bill, *Draft Modern Slavery Bill*, House of Lords Paper No. 166, House of Commons Paper No. 1019, Session 2013–14 (2014) (*'the Joint Committee Report'*).
38 Ibid 87 [175].
39 *Transparency in Supply Chains etc. A Practical Guide* (Home Office, London, 2018) 10 [4.3] (*'Transparency in Supply Chains'*), referring to the *Companies Act 2006* (UK) c. 46, Ch 4A, s 414C (*'Companies Act'*).

In reality, modern slavery statements and action plans may differ considerably from audit-style reporting, since the stated purpose of the Strategic Report is 'to inform members of the company and help them assess how the directors have performed their duty ... to promote the success of the company'.[40] In the end, the Joint Committee did recommend amending the *Companies Act* so that the requirement to report on 'social, community and human rights issues' in a Strategic Report specifically included modern slavery.[41] This requirement did not eventuate.

The Joint Committee discussed supply chains but left some important matters open.[42]

Recognising the global nature of the problem, and the 'length and complexity of major companies' supply chains',[43] effective action required a wider approach. While recognising the valuable role of voluntary actions and the work of NGOs in raising awareness of the problem of modern slavery in supply chains, the Joint Committee did not think this was 'enough to ensure that all companies take the necessary steps to eradicate slavery from their supply chains'.[44]

Legislating for supply chains was clearly needed to level the playing field, but companies also benefited financially from ethical conduct, according to witnesses,[45] who said they could 'support legislation that was not unduly burdensome'.[46] The Joint Committee welcomed business support and called on the Government to follow suit in its own procurement.[47]

The Bribery Act model was not recommended. It was 'tricky', onerous and complex, resulting in burdensome compliance, even if companies utilised an existing structure.[48]

After reviewing the Californian legislation,[49] the Joint Committee noted that 'some companies had exceeded the reporting requirements and were keen to demonstrate progress over time'.[50] While this may not have occurred without the Act, which 'had helped to raise consumer,

---

40 *Companies Act*, Ch 4A, s 414C.
41 Ibid s 414C(7)(a)(iii).
42 *Joint Committee Report*, above n 37, 85–92.
43 Ibid 85 [166].
44 Ibid 86 [170].
45 Ibid 86–7 [171]–[172].
46 Ibid 87 [172].
47 Ibid 87 [173].
48 Ibid 87 [174]–[175].
49 *California Transparency Act*.
50 *Joint Committee Report*, above n 37, 88 [177], quoting US Ambassador-at-Large Luis CdeBaca.

investor and business awareness of modern slavery issues', adoption of a similar regime was not universally popular with witnesses, because that would add an additional level of reporting. In addition, the 'fit' of this stand-alone legislation within the proposed UK Act was not assured.[51]

The Joint Committee thought that adding a modern slavery element to current *Companies Act* reporting[52] would be a 'straightforward' way to 'build on existing reporting'; it was widely supported by business witnesses, and should be done,[53] and that the Secretary of State specify by Order what was to be included.[54] The advantages were: clarity about which companies must comply; building on an existing process without adding an extra reporting burden on those already tackling the system, and at the same time forcing other companies to start addressing the problem; allowing easy identification of ethical companies by stakeholders (NGOs, consumers and investors).[55]

While accepting the merit of making individual non-executive directors responsible for a company's annual modern slavery statement, the Joint Committee had 'no desire to reverse some of the effective alternative approaches some companies have already adopted' or add extra burdens. In addition, it could be counterproductive by diminishing group accountability within a company. However, holding CEOs accountable was desirable. The question was left to the recommended statutory review stage.[56]

Notably, while the PLS Committee had welcomed the creation of an Anti-Slavery Commissioner,[57] the Joint Committee went further, pressing for greater statutory guarantees of the independence of that office as well as a greatly expanded, overarching role that would encompass victim protection, management of statistics and other

---

51 Ibid 88 [178].
52 By amending Section 414C (7) of the *Companies Act*.
53 *Joint Committee Report*, above n 37, 88–9 [179]–[180].
54 Ibid 89 [184]:

> …These requirements must include explanations of how the company has, with respect to modern slavery: (a) verified its supply chains to evaluate and address risks; (b) audited suppliers; (c) certified goods and services purchased from suppliers; (d) maintained internal accountability standards, and (e) trained staff. The Order should also require that this information is published online.

55 Ibid 89 [181].
56 Ibid 90 [185]–[187].
57 The Home Office had included this in the draft Modern Slavery Bill published in December 2013.

information (collection, compilation, analysis and dissemination) and a role in building national and international partnerships.[58]

3.4 The government's response

On 10 June 2014, the Government issued a 30-page response[59] to the Joint Committee report in which supply chains were covered in less than two pages.

While recognising the 'global nature of modern slavery', it was unwilling to follow the Joint Committee's recommendation to further amend the *Companies Act* and to require companies to identify an individual with responsibility at board level as initial steps. The Government stressed the vital role played by the private sector both to ensure their supply chains were free from exploitation and to take action in mitigation. For its own part, the Government said it had already taken 'a number of steps' to 'raise awareness among the private sector'. It adverted to the strategic statement that had been required by the *Companies Act* since October 2013, where there was some expectation, but no requirement, that supply chains might be reported on:[60]

> UK quoted companies have had to report on human rights, 'where relevant for an understanding of the business'. This is a new reporting requirement and so it is too early to say whether human rights reporting is effective and sufficient when it comes to the inclusion of disclosures on slavery.

In addition, work being done at EU level was likely to be enacted in 2016, and these arrangements would 'go further than the current Companies Act requirements' by extending to 'business relationships' including subcontractors and suppliers.

At that point, the Government baulked at further action:[61]

> the Government is ... mindful of existing requirements on business and possible future changes to the business reporting regime

---

58 *Joint Committee Report*, above n 37, 78–84.
59 *The Government Response to the Report from the Joint committee On the Draft Modern Slavery Bill Session 2013–14 HL Paper 166 / HC 1019*, 23 ('*the Government Response*'): draft Modern Slavery Bill, Presented to Parliament by the Secretary of State for the Home Department by Command of Her Majesty June 2014.
60 Ibid 22.
61 Ibid.

[and] wants to work collaboratively with businesses to support them to eliminate forced labour in supply chains, in a way which does not place additional burdens on them.

This response was framed as building on the existing legislative framework and consulting with business 'to establish what more can be done to raise awareness among their workforce and their sub-contractors, and develop an evidence base on best practice'.[62]

The Government stressed the complexity of supply chain issues[63] and the 'diminished influence' of UK-based companies in overseas contexts. Bringing businesses together 'to discuss the challenges and opportunities in tackling modern slavery in supply chains' was the Government's committed approach.[64]

In relation to the Gangmasters Licensing Authority, the Government agreed that there was 'scope to review some of its powers, remit and structures' but was 'pleased that the report recognises that any extension to the remit of the GLA would have an impact on its limited resources'. The course of action[65] it took was to transfer sponsorship of the authority to the Home Office[66] to 'improve collaboration with policing agencies for its enforcement activities'.[67]

> The Home Office is considering the other issues for review raised by the report, bearing in mind that there may be more effective ways to achieve improvements without regulating to increase the GLA's licensing remit into other sectors.

The response also noted the expanding role of the Anti-Slavery Commissioner role since the PLS Committee report, as demonstrated by the Joint Committee's expanded view of the role.[68]

The Government committed itself 'to providing a Post-Legislative Scrutiny memorandum on the Bill within three to five years of Royal Assent' but would 'consult the Home Affairs Committee on the timing of publication of the memorandum'.[69]

---

62 Ibid 23.
63 As it continued to do throughout the Committee Debates discussed at Section 3.6 below.
64 *Government Response*, above n 59, 23.
65 Ibid: announced by the Prime Minister on 9 April 2014.
66 Ibid: from the Department for Environment, Food & Rural Affairs.
67 Ibid.
68 Ibid 12.
69 Ibid 30.

3.5 Early progression of the Bill through Parliament

3.5.1 First stage, June and July 2014

The UK House of Commons Bill was presented[70] and given its First Reading on 10 June 2014.[71] It was presented as 'a Bill to make provision about slavery, servitude and forced or compulsory labour; to make provision about human trafficking; to make provision for an Anti-slavery Commissioner; and for connected purposes'. It did not contain any specific reference to supply chains.

The Second Reading took place on 8 July,[72] along with the related Money Resolution[73] and Programme motion.[74]

3.6 The Committee debates (Commons)

The legislation now moved to the Committee stage. Over 11 separate sittings, the Bill was debated in Committee in the House of Commons.

3.6.1 First Sitting

At the first Committee debate, on 21 July 2014,[75] the Public Bill Committee agreed to a further programme motion to sit in private, to take written evidence that would be reported to the House, and to examine witnesses.[76] The session dealt extensively with the supply chain issue,

---

70 By Theresa May, Secretary, supported by the Prime Minister, the Deputy Prime Minister, Mr Chancellor of the Exchequer, Iain Duncan Smith, Secretary, Chris Grayling, Secretary and Karen Bradley, Parliamentary Under-Secretary of State for the Home Department.
71 United Kingdom, *Parliamentary Debates*, House of Commons, 10 June 2014, vol 582 col 413 (Theresa May).
72 United Kingdom, *Parliamentary Debates*, House of Commons, 8 July 2014, vol 584 col 166 (Theresa May).
73 Ibid col 206.
74 Ibid.
75 Public Bill Committee, *Parliamentary Debates: Modern Slavery Bill*, First Sitting, House of Commons, Bill No. 008, Session 2014–15 (2014).
76 Ibid: Witnesses commenting on supply chain issues were: Alison Saunders, Director of Public Prosecutions; Ian Cruxton, Director of Organised Crime Command, National Crime Agency; Dr Charles Reed, Foreign Policy Adviser, Church of England (lead official on migration policy); Cecilia Taylor-Camara, Head of the Bishops Conference Office for Migration Policy, Catholic Bishops for England and Wales; Lucy Maule, Senior Researcher, Centre for Social Justice (former specialist adviser to the Joint Committee on the draft Modern Slavery Bill); Andrew Wallis, Chief Executive Officer, Unseen UK; Kate Roberts, Community Advocate,

driven in particular by Michael Connarty MP, who asked witnesses whether the Bill should include a mandatory, rather than a voluntary, measure on corporate supply chains.[77]

Peter Carter, the specialist barrister who had advised the Joint Committee and had pressed the Bribery Act model, continued to support it in preference to the Californian supply chain transparency model, as a signal of 'how importantly it is regarded – by creating a criminal offence':[78]

> The California model is a good model. The alternative, which the Joint Committee proposed, was having a requirement to report, which is a starting point, but I do not see why companies should be regarded as having a less onerous obligation [in modern slavery than] over money laundering or corruption.[79]

Other witnesses agreed that mandatory compliance, with criminal sanctions, was necessary.[80] Church representatives wanted a supply chain provision, but noted the global complexity of supply chains, and the need to address the causes of the problem;[81] they appeared satisfied with a light-touch approach to start with.[82]

Andrew Wallis MP[83] stressed the importance of business attitudes and the need to have a level playing field:

Kalayaan; Nadine Finch, Garden Court Chambers (barrister, expert and consultant in human trafficking and children's rights); Peter Carter QC, Red Lion Chambers (barrister, specialising in prosecutions, former specialist adviser to the Joint Committee on the draft Modern Slavery Bill).

77 Ibid col 31, Q 63.
78 Ibid col 31, Q 80. The model was also supported by Anti-Slavery International.
79 Ibid.
80 Ibid col 31, Q 63: per Andrew Wallis (CEO of Unseen), Lucy Maule (Senior Researcher, Centre for Social Justice and former specialist adviser to the Joint Committee) and Kate Roberts (community advocate).
81 Ibid Qs 25–6, 31 and 42: Charles Reed wished to make supply chains a priority.
82 Ibid Qs 25–6: Cecilia Taylor-Camara, who espoused a Fair Trade model, also cited the US *Business Supply Chain Transparency on Trafficking and Slavery Act of 2014*, 'which requires "companies with annual worldwide gross receipts exceeding one hundred million dollars" to put in an annual report to the Securities and Exchange Commission any efforts they are making to address [modern slavery] in their supply chains'; however, this draft legislation, reconsidered by Congress in 2015, did not pass into law. This has been reintroduced on 23 October 2018 (as of 25 July 2019, not yet passed).
83 Ibid Q 59: Andrew Wallis.

At the moment, we have a prosecution Bill with a little bit of prevention, and nothing about partnership. Business is not seen anywhere. The truth is that NGOs and Government are broke. The issues around business, and the vulnerability in its supply chains and practices, are huge and are recognised globally. Businesses want to see Government taking a lead on this issue. They want a level playing field. More and more businesses are starting to come forward [and will pressure the Government].

Wallis disagreed with the pre-legislative Committee's recommendation to add any provision to the *Companies Act*, 'because there is a real danger that you will end up penalising just British businesses, and you will not catch private businesses'. All businesses operating in the UK over a threshold limit 'should start disclosing what they are doing', and there was great commercial advantage in advertising compliance.[84]

At the conclusion of the session, the matter was adjourned until Tuesday 2 September 2014.

3.6.2 Second and Third Sittings

The Committee did not discuss supply chains in the Second Sitting,[85] but at the Third Sitting[86] Members discussed Amendments 41 and 54, introduced by David Burrowes MP (Conservative), which related to proposed extensions of trafficking and slavery offences to include supply chain elements and 'spell out more clearly that trafficking can involve many people at different stages'.[87]

Labour MP Diana Johnson spoke briefly to Amendment 54 (seeking to extend the scope of 'exploitation' in Clause 3) in order to 'establish the principle that supply chains are an important part of our response ... and they need to be a part of our deliberations'. The Opposition saw 'the absence of any measure in the Bill to deal with supply chains' as 'one of its biggest failings', a sentiment which 'many members of the Committee feel it is important to address'.[88]

---

84 Ibid.
85 In the morning of 2 September 2014.
86 In the afternoon of 2 September 2014.
87 Public Bill Committee, *Parliamentary Debates: Modern Slavery Bill*, Third Sitting, House of Commons, Bill No. 008, Session 2014–15 (2014) cols 108–20: amendments 41 and 54, which were dealt with together. They were ultimately withdrawn.
88 Ibid col 110.

After citing shocking examples from business, Johnson reminded members of the submission from 'the Ethical Trading Initiative, including the 80 corporate members, who are campaigning for legislation on supply chains to be included in the Bill', and stated that 'a clear 82% of the UK public believe that there should be legislation to govern supply chains. The charity sector is equally clear'.[89] The size of reporting companies, the content of the reports, their method of dissemination and enforcement all needed to be discussed and settled.[90] Sir Andrew Stunell again pressed for a small amendment to the *Companies Act*, noting that the supply chain issue was clearly a missing element in the Bill.[91] He persisted in seeking 'just ... some simple wording to be added that says, "including the impact of their supply chain on those issues". That is not onerous'.[92] Michael Connarty MP (Labour) also pressed the case for supply chain measures.[93]

However, Karen Bradley,[94] expressing the Government's determination to work with business and obtain more evidence that would make legislated solutions effective in what were very complex situations,[95] stressed that she was working with business and that supply chains would be dealt with further down the track:[96]

> I am working on that to ensure that we have an approach that enables business to take the action that we need in a way that works. It would be a waste if we spent a lot of time doing something that does not get the result we want ... Obviously, we will discuss the matter of transparency in supply chains later in the Committee ... [so] if any of the amendments are put to a Division, I urge members of the Committee to reject that Division while we are still working on the evidence we need.

The likelihood that the Bill would increase opportunities for local community campaigns such as '[i]f you see something, say something' was noted.[97] However, in the face of the Government's assurances that

---

89 Ibid col 111.
90 Ibid col 112.
91 Ibid col 113 (being an amendment to *Companies Act 2006* (UK), Chapter 4A, s 414C, as the Joint Committee had recommended).
92 Ibid col 119.
93 Ibid cols 114–15.
94 In the course of discussing amendments 41 and 54.
95 Public Bill Committee, *Parliamentary Debates: Modern Slavery Bill*, Third Sitting, House of Commons, Bill No. 008, Session 2014–15 (2014) col 118.
96 Ibid col 119–20.
97 Ibid cols 114, 120 (Michael Connarty).

the offences set out in the Bill were effective in their current form, and that the Government was determined not to act 'precipitously' on the supply chain issue, but rather to shape a response in partnership with business, Mr Burrowes withdrew:[98]

> It was ... helpful to hear early salvos on the transparency of supply chains debate and to see how we are inching along in that direction. I look forward to an earnest debate when scrutinising that matter, and what the Government come back with when we get to it. On that basis, I beg to ask leave to withdraw the amendment.

3.6.3 Fourth and Fifth Sittings

At the Fourth and Fifth Sittings on the morning and afternoon of 4 September 2014,[99] the Committee debated the details of trafficking clauses, child trafficking, exploitation and penalties. Again Karen Bradley, Parliamentary Under-Secretary of State for the Home Department, pressed members to withdraw their proposed amendments so that the Bill could be passed expeditiously:[100]

> My focus at the moment is entirely on modern slavery and ensuring that the Modern Slavery Bill becomes an Act of Parliament. That is what I spend most of my waking moments doing. I know that the words of the hon. Lady and other Committee members are on the record and have been heard and considered by people outside this room. [However] Clause 5 [is effective as it stands]. Our approach to penalties for those who commit modern slavery is clear ... Strengthening our sentencing powers for modern slavery offences will send a strong signal to those thinking of getting involved in slavery and trafficking that the UK will not tolerate any form of abuse or exploitation of others.

Thus, on all matters, proposed amendments to the penalty provisions were withdrawn or voted down along party lines.

---

98 Ibid col 120.
99 Public Bill Committee, *Parliamentary Debates: Modern Slavery Bill*, Fourth Sitting, House of Commons, Bill No. 008, Session 2014–15 (2014); Public Bill Committee, *Parliamentary Debates: Modern Slavery Bill*, Fifth Sitting, House of Commons, Bill No. 008, Session 2014–15 (2014).
100 Public Bill Committee, *Parliamentary Debates: Modern Slavery Bill*, Fifth Sitting, House of Commons, Bill No. 008, Session 2014–15 (2014) col 205.

3.6.4 Sixth and Seventh Sittings

The Sixth and Seventh Sittings, which dealt with responses to the modern slavery offences themselves, and legal responses to them, took place on the morning and afternoon, respectively, of 9 September 2014.[101] There was no discussion of supply chains, but the independence of the Anti-Slavery Commissioner came sharply into focus in the Seventh Session. Michael Connarty pressed for the word 'independent' to be inserted in the Bill, but the Government resisted.[102] The genuine independence of the Commissioner remained an unresolved issue, and in due course, it led to the resignation of the first person to hold that office.[103]

3.6.5 Eighth and Ninth Sittings

In the Eighth and Ninth Sittings of the Committee on 11 September 2014, supply chains were mentioned only in passing, in relation to the independence of the Anti-Slavery Commissioner.[104] As it turned out, this topic of constant contention remains unresolved.

3.6.6 Tenth and Eleventh Sittings

In the morning of 14 October 2014, the Tenth Sitting of the Committee dealt with other matters. However, the final, Eleventh Sitting, in the afternoon, marked a shift in the Government's willingness to proceed with supply chain issues. The Committee debated a group of measures including Sir Andrew Stunell's proposed new Clause 25, which would make the small *Companies Act* amendment suggested by the Joint

---

101 Public Bill Committee, *Parliamentary Debates: Modern Slavery Bill*, Sixth Sitting, House of Commons, Bill No. 008, Session 2014–15 (2014); Public Bill Committee, *Parliamentary Debates: Modern Slavery Bill*, Seventh Sitting, House of Commons, Bill No. 008, Session 2014–15 (2014).
102 Public Bill Committee, *Parliamentary Debates: Modern Slavery Bill*, Seventh Sitting, House of Commons, Bill No. 008, Session 2014–15 (2014) col 308: Karen Bradley said,

> it would be negligent of me, as a Minister, to agree to put the word "independent" in the Bill until I have checked – as I have committed to doing, because I understand the strength of feeling in Committee – that to make such a change would have no unintended consequences.

103 See Lizzie Deardon, *UK's First Independent Anti-Slavery Commissioner Resigns Citing Government Interference* (17 May 2018) The Independent <www.independent.co.uk/news/uk/politics/modern-slavery-uk-commissioner-resigns-interference-kevin-hyland-government-a8356601.html>.
104 Public Bill Committee, *Parliamentary Debates: Modern Slavery Bill*, Eighth Sitting, House of Commons, Bill No. 008, Session 2014–15 (2014) col 338.

Committee in its report.[105] The proposed amendment was brought up, and read for the first time, together with discussion on proposed new Clauses 32 (disclosure by companies of the measures they had taken to eradicate offences from their supply chains); 33 (banning importation of products produced by slavery or forced labour); 34 (legal liability for the beneficiaries of slavery); and 36 (large UK companies' duty to report efforts to eradicate modern slavery and forced labour).

Members agreed that supply chain issues were the most glaring omission in the Bill when it was first published.[106] However, on 13 October the Minister had written to the Chairs of the Committee that she would look at bringing forward amendments to require businesses above a certain size to disclose what they have done to ensure there is no modern slavery in their supply chains.[107] Sir Andrew Stunell agreed to withdraw his *Companies Act* proposal:

> Given that [the Minister] has outlined a series of proposals that go beyond those in my new clause, it would be folly for me to do anything other than to withdraw it. I hope very much that the Government will deliver on all that she has promised. I beg to ask leave to withdraw the motion.

The point had now been reached where supply chain transparency through reporting would be seriously addressed. Under time pressure, at the end of the session, Karen Bradley undertook to carry the supply chain measures forward 'on report' (at the report stage):[108]

> I believe that we can now bring forward a simple but effective provision on Report that will require businesses to produce a disclosure

---

105 That is, amending the *Companies Act* to include a requirement for companies to refer in their annual reports to their modern slavery statement.
106 Public Bill Committee, *Parliamentary Debates: Modern Slavery Bill*, Eleventh Sitting, House of Commons, Bill No. 008, Session 2014–15 (2014) cols 483–5 (Andrew Stunell and Diana Johnson).
107 Ibid col 493:

> Following my letter yesterday, Members will be aware that the Government intend to bring forward a disclosure requirement on Report. That is a big step forward. It also reflects my discussions with members of this Committee and the important evidence gathered by the pre-legislative scrutiny Committee.
>
> (Karen Bradley)

108 Ibid col 494. The consultation framed choice between £36m, £100m, £250m, and £1bn. 80% of 84 responses selected £36m. See Modern Slavery and Supply Chains Government Response, *Summary of Consultation Responses and Next Steps* (Home Office, July 20015) 7.

> each year setting out what they have done to eradicate modern slavery from their supply chain. Our initial thinking is that that will apply to larger companies. However, we want to get the threshold right. We intend to consult ... The detail about the level of the threshold would then be set by secondary legislation ... We also intend to produce statutory guidance to accompany this provision ... [and] We intend to consult on this guidance before it is finished.

Thus, the Government made its first commitment to the enactment of a reporting regime with similarities to the Californian *Transparency in Supply Chains Act*. With the benefit of California's experience, the UK Government believed that 'in some respects our measure will go further';[109] its scope would be expanded beyond businesses that provide goods for sale to include service providers. However, the *Companies Act* amendments would not be made:[110]

> ...one of the key reasons that we have decided to introduce a stand-alone measure is that the Companies Act applies only to publicly listed companies ... [and] Our measure will require all companies over a certain size to disclose what they are doing to ensure that there is no slavery in their supply chains.

The Bill, as amended in other areas, was then to be reported to the House. On Report, the Government included the new clause on supply chains for debate.

3.6.7 *The report stage and Third Reading in the Commons*

On 4 November 2014, the Bill passed through its Report and Third Reading[111] stages in the House of Commons, along with the necessary Programme Motion (No 2)[112] for the Bill's advancement in its amended form, to include the new reporting regime that would become Section 54 of the Act when passed. The amended Bill was read the First time and was to be read a second time on Friday 23 January 2015, and to be printed (Bill 112).[113]

---

109 Ibid.
110 Ibid.
111 United Kingdom, *Parliamentary Debates*, House of Commons, 4 November 2014, vol 587 col 789 (Theresa May).
112 Ibid col 682.
113 Ibid cols 721–59.

While the Commissioner's independence had been added to the Act, the method of appointment remained vexed, as pinpointed by Mr Burrowes:[114]

> The amendment that provides that the anti-slavery commissioner is independent is a welcome addition to the Bill. Will the fact that they are now explicitly independent under the Bill affect the selection process, which I understand has already started with the advertising of the position?
> Mrs May: It was always the intention that the anti-slavery commissioner would be independent and that does not affect the selection process ... I assure my hon. Friend that [nobody] has ever suggested that the appointment by the Home Secretary of the chief inspector of borders and immigration leads to him being anything other than extremely independent in his reports.

With hindsight, this turned out not to be the case.

3.7 The House of Lords

On 5 November 2014, the Bill was read for the first time in the House of Lords.[115]

3.7.1 Second Reading: House of Lords

On 17 November 2014, a total of 31 speakers were listed for the Second Reading of the Modern Slavery Bill, with Back-Bench contributions being kept to eight minutes to allow Lord Bates' committal motion to be put at approximately 8 pm.[116]

At this stage,[117] Lord Alton raised the supply chain amendments championed by Baroness Kennedy and the need for a post-legislative review:[118]

> it seems that the proverbial words about the curate's egg apply to the Bill: it is good in parts; there is much to commend, but there

---

114 Ibid col 791.
115 Some amendments were made: United Kingdom, *Parliamentary Debates*, House of Lords, 5 November 2014, vol 756 col 1621.
116 United Kingdom, *Parliamentary Debates*, House of Lords, 17 November 2014, vol 757 col 237 (Arrangement of Business).
117 Ibid col 284.
118 Ibid. See also col 286.

is still work to be done ... a sunset clause requiring us to return to this Bill in a relatively short time—let us say, three years—to look again at how it has worked, on everything from the anti-slavery commissioner to supply chain transparency and victim support, should be put in the Bill.

After speeches, the Bill was duly read a second time and committed to a Committee of the Whole House of Lords.

3.7.2 The Committee debates (Lords)

On 1 December, the House of Lords sat for the first day in Committee.[119] Supply chain matters were not considered. Meanwhile, on 29 November 2014, the UK's Modern Slavery Strategy had been published, setting out a 'comprehensive cross-government approach to fighting modern slavery, based on four Ps – Pursue, Prevent, Protect and Prepare'.[120] The Strategy made clear that there were many more victims than were initially envisaged.

The advisability of publishing the strategy before the legislation was finalised was raised in the House of Lords,[121] and consistency was noted as a potential issue. The need for the strategy to be iterative and responsive was first hinted at in this context:

> My noble friend Lady Hamwee asked a very pertinent question, which sent a flood of notes back and forth to and from the Bill team, on whether the strategy document, on which the ink is yet to dry, is open to amendment. You could see officials wincing at the prospect, but this is something that needs to be kept under review. I refer my noble friend to Clause 42, which refers to the role of the anti-slavery commissioner and his requirement to produce strategic plans and annual reports; those reports will come before Parliament and we will have an opportunity to discuss them.

---

119 United Kingdom, *Parliamentary Debates*, House of Lords, 1 December 2014, vol 757 col 1114 (First Sitting discussing amendments related to victims, including children, and their support).
120 See *Modern Slavery Strategy* (Policy Paper, Home Office, 29 November 2014).
121 United Kingdom, *Parliamentary Debates*, House of Lords, 1 December 2014, vol 757 col 1136.

Baroness Hamwee[122] had wanted a review of various matters[123] after one year; Baroness Royall echoed Baroness Hamwee's concern about the strategy, but argued that one year was 'too tight' and proposed review 'in due course'.[124] Baroness Howarth thought a legislatively mandated review essential, but more appropriately set at 18 months to two years.[125]

The upshot was that the Government considered review important, and would commit to it in a general way, but not at a specific point in time. Lord Bates placed on record the Government's commitment to undertake a review within three to five years.[126]

On the morning of 3 December 2014, the House of Lords sat in Committee for its Second Sitting.[127] It was not until the Third Sitting, on 8 December, that supply chain reporting was raised.[128] Baroness Cox approved the global dimension that was now featured in the Government's strategy, but noted the absence of supply chain measures:[129]

> the Bill as it stands falls far short of these commitments ... It currently focuses ... on various forms of slavery within the UK. Clearly, the very important issue of supply chains addresses an international dimension of exploitation and servitude related to UK-based companies ... there is currently nothing [else] in the Bill that recognises and begins to address the many other forms of slavery around the world ....

Baroness Butler-Sloss[130] commended the supply chain amendment in her name: 'My Amendment 67ZC deals with the supply chain. It is splendid—the Government are to be congratulated on it; they talk

---

122 Ibid 1128–30: speaking to proposed amendment 100.
123 Ibid: Including other related legislation.
124 Ibid col 1131.
125 Ibid col 1134.
126 Ibid col 1137.
127 United Kingdom, *Parliamentary Debates*, House of Lords, 3 December 2014, vol 757 col 1345 (Second Sitting).
128 United Kingdom, *Parliamentary Debates*, House of Lords, 8 December 2014, vol 757 col 1610 (Third Sitting).
129 Ibid col 1617.
130 Ibid col 1620.

about the necessity for companies to check right down the ladder and to write reports'. However, she notes[131]

> nothing at the moment in that part of the Bill says who should monitor it. My amendment would allow the commissioner to have oversight and a monitoring role. I also suggested, perhaps slightly cheekily, that he should have the power to impose penalties. I am not sure whether the commissioner will have that power, but we have not yet heard from the Government who will impose penalties if companies are not prepared to obey ....

Baroness Butler-Sloss argued that the Commissioner should receive copies of statements and also have a duty to collect data (something that was not yet in the Bill).

Lord Deben[132] pressed the Minister to consider ways in which the Commissioner could be made fully independent:

> It is of considerable importance to your independence that you are seen not as a departmental subject but as open to advising the Government as a whole. I therefore hope that the Government will look again at exactly how the terms of the relationships between the Home Office and the commissioner are drawn.

On 10 December 2014, in its Fourth Committee Sitting,[133] the House of Lords considered an amendment to the supply chain provisions now set out in Clause 51, seeking to make specific reporting information mandatory and to set out the steps taken by the organisation. Lord Bates referred to the Government's role as a procurer.[134] Lord Rosser stressed the need for public information:[135]

> enough information needs to be required in the statement to enable a consumer, a voluntary organisation or the media to form a view on how well or otherwise a company is doing ... Frankly, the Minister has not said anything to provide me with any comfort that the Government intend to include anything in the Bill that will ensure that the necessary information is provided to enable those meaningful comparisons to be made.

---

131 Ibid.
132 Ibid col 1627: Lord Deben is a Conservative.
133 United Kingdom, *Parliamentary Debates*, House of Lords, 10 December 2014, vol 757 col 1836.
134 Ibid col 1890.
135 Ibid col 1892.

Lord Bates, having carriage of the Bill in the Lords, stated the Government's position and asked Lord Rosser to withdraw his proposed amendment in light of continuing consultation.[136] With regret, Lord Rosser acquiesced and withdrew the amendment and Clause 51 was agreed.

Lord Alton moved another amendment to the supply chain provisions;[137] it was in terms similar to the Act as ultimately passed, and he received support; as he put it, 'That is what these amendments seek to do—they put real flesh on the bones of Clause 51'. However, reluctantly accepting the Government's pressure, he, too withdrew his amendment.[138] After debate on other matters, the Lords adjourned.

On 23 and 25 February 2015, the House of Lords considered the Bill at Report stage, in its First and Second Sittings, respectively. On 23 February, Lord Bates observed,[139]

> Many changes were made in the other place. Between consideration in the other place and here, the Government added the new clause on the supply chain and during the detailed process we went through in Committee, 23 amendments were tabled. There was then an extensive period of meetings with interested Members of the House of Lords. The level of engagement, not only from Peers but from NGOs and charities that work in this area and have deep concerns, was incredibly impressive and helpful. They brought their expertise, and we were able to hear from the Independent Anti-slavery Commissioner, who gave us an insight into how he sees his role. As a result, the Government have tabled a record number, I think, of amendments—72—which we will go through. I set that out as context to show that there is cross-party commitment to see this legislation on the statute book as soon as possible to make sure that victims are protected and that law enforcement agencies have the powers they need to be able to tackle people who are guilty of these crimes.

In the face of this extensive reshaping, which included many of their own contributions, other Lords withdrew their individual amendments. On 25 February, the Government, through Lord Bates, moved Amendment 97 to the Bill, concerning the contents that an

---

136 Ibid col 1891.
137 Ibid col 1892–3: amendment 98.
138 Ibid col 1907.
139 United Kingdom, *Parliamentary Debates*, House of Lords, 23 February 2015, vol 759 col 1413.

54 Modern Slavery Act UK

organisation's statement 'may include'.[140] Other minor amendments were agreed.

On 4 March 2015, the Third Reading took place in the House of Lords.[141] Lord Alton moved an amendment to establish a central repository for slavery and human trafficking statements.[142] Despite the support, the Government again cited the need for consultations, to which Lord Alton responded,

> The noble Lord has told us that we should wait for a consultation, but I cannot think of an organisation ... that we would consult about this proposal that has not already come out in favour of a central repository.[143]

However, there was a Division on the amendment, and it was disagreed along party lines.

3.8 Final stages and assent

On 17 March 2015, the Commons received the Lords' Report and final amendments but did not agree to them.[144] The Programme motion for the Bill in its final amended form was passed on 17 March 2015 in the House of Commons, in the form preferred by the Commons.[145]

The Government members stressed that it was:[146]

> essential that we get this Bill on the statute book before the Dissolution of Parliament next week. Although the amendments coming from the other place ... have absolutely the right sentiment ... it is vital that we ensure this legislation gets on the statute book

---

140 United Kingdom, *Parliamentary Debates*, House of Lords, 25 February 2015, vol 759 col 1750.
141 United Kingdom, *Parliamentary Debates*, House of Lords, 4 March 2015, vol 760 col 221.
142 Ibid col 229.
143 Ibid col 239–40.
144 United Kingdom, *Parliamentary Debates*, House of Commons, 17 March 2015, vol 594 col 645 (Programme No. 3). Amendments were suggested to Clauses 1, 2, 8, 10, 13, 30, 34, 37, 40–3 and 45. No amendments regarding the supply chain transparency provision. See Lords Amendments to Modern Slavery Bill 184, Session 2014–15 (6 March 2015).
145 Ibid.
146 Ibid col 646: Henry Smith (Conservative), asking a 'Dorothy Dix' question.

at the earliest possible opportunity so that these fundamental and important protections can become the law of the land.

The Minister readily agreed:[147]

> He is right: we are at a very late stage and we want this Bill to become an Act of Parliament. We want the Modern Slavery Act, the first piece of anti-slavery legislation for 200 years, to be on the statute book. We must make sure we achieve that ....

The final form of the Bill approved by the Commons returned to the Lords on 25 March 2015,[148] where no further amendments proposed by the Lords were passed. Accordingly, the Bill in the form preferred by the Commons on 17 March proceeded.

On 26 March 2015 the *Modern Slavery Act* received Royal Assent and on 29 Oct 2015 Regulations were approved and the Government's guidance was published.

3.9 The 2017 proposed amendments

In 2016, Theresa May commissioned an independent review from barrister Caroline Haughey, who found, according to May, that:[149]

> there has been good progress in the first year of the act, with 289 modern slavery offences prosecuted in 2015 alone and a 40% rise in the number of victims identified by the State [but] there is still further to go on raising awareness ... improving training ... and strengthening support for victims [and that] the response of local police forces can be too patchy.

---

147 Ibid.
148 United Kingdom, *Parliamentary Debates*, House of Lords, 25 March 2015, vol 760 col 1426: Motion A Moved by Lord Bates, 'That this House do not insist on its Amendment 72 and do agree with the Commons in their Amendments 72A, 72B and 72C in lieu' was passed.
149 Theresa May, *My Government Will Lead the Way in Defeating Modern Slavery* (Sunday Telegraph) 30 July 2016 <https://www.telegraph.co.uk/news/2016/07/30/we-will-lead-the-way-in-defeating-modern-slavery/>; republished as *Defeating Modern Slavery: article by Theresa May* (31 July 2016) UK Government <https://www.gov.uk/government/speeches/defeating-modern-slavery-theresa-may-article>. The article was republished in glowing terms: 'how her government will lead the way in defeating modern slavery'.

May stressed the importance of working 'collaboratively with law-enforcement agencies across the world to track and stop these pernicious gangs who operate across borders and jurisdictions'.[150]

In the Government's own assessment, the *Modern Slavery Act 2015*:[151]

> has delivered enhanced protection and support for victims and a world-leading transparency requirement on businesses to show that modern slavery is not taking place in their companies or their supply chains.

A Private Members Bill sponsored by Baroness Young of Hornsey was introduced in the House of Lords on 12 July 2017, when it received a First Reading (as usual, a formality). The important debating stage that accompanies a Second Reading has not yet occurred.[152] The purpose of the Bill is to amend the *Modern Slavery Act* (UK) to require mandatory coverage of topic areas in statements,[153] and if the company reports that no steps have been taken, explain why;[154] to bring public agencies within the regime;[155] and to require the Secretary of State to publish a list of all commercial organisations that are required to publish a statement.[156]

3.10 The 2018 review

After three years, the shape of the regime in operation is emerging – incidentally, the same timeframe that was selected in Australia as the appropriate period to allow before a mandatory review.[157] In July 2018, at the request of the Prime Minister, the Home Secretary announced a formal review of the Act.[158]

The review was to be (and was) completed by the end of March 2019, with a final report tabled in Parliament on 22 May 2019. The UK Government responded to the recommendations arising from the review in July 2019.

150 Ibid.
151 Ibid.
152 Or been scheduled (as at 31 July 2019).
153 Modern Slavery (Transparency in Supply Chains) Bill [HL] 2017, s 1(4).
154 Ibid s 1(3).
155 Ibid s 1(2).
156 Ibid s 1(5).
157 See discussion in Chapter 4.
158 Frank Field, Maria Miller, Elizabeth Butler-Sloss, *Independent Review of the Modern Slavery Act 2015, Final Report*, 11 ('*Independent Review*').

Modern Slavery Act UK 57

The review examined four areas: Independent Anti-Slavery Commissioner; transparency in supply chains; independent child trafficking advocates; and the legal application of the Act.[159] In relation to transparency in supply chains, which is the focus of this chapter, the review addressed the question: 'how to ensure compliance and drive up the quality of [slavery and human trafficking] statements produced by eligible companies'.[160] It presented findings and made recommendations in seven areas:[161]

- **Clarifying which companies are in scope** by establishing an internal Government list of companies that fall within the scope of Section 54. The companies themselves should remain responsible for reporting, and non-inclusion in the list should not be an excuse not to comply.[162] The UK Government accepted this recommendation.[163]
- **Improving the quality of statements** in six ways. Four are discussed further below. The two more minor ones were to strengthen the statutory guidance to include a template covering information in each of the six areas,[164] and that the Independent Anti-Slavery Commissioner should oversee the guidance available to companies.[165] The UK Government accepted the template recommendation and committed to including a template in updated statutory guidance to be published in 2020.[166] However, the UK Government disagreed with the Independent Anti-Slavery Commissioner overseeing the statutory guidance, clearly stating that responsibility lay with the Home Secretary.[167]
- **Embedding modern slavery reporting into business culture** by tying it more directly to company law reporting requirements[168] and

---

159 *Independent Review*, above n 158, 11. In relation to the legal application of the Act, the review considered the definition of 'exploitation' (s 3), reparation orders (s 8–10) and the statutory defence (s 45).
160 Ibid 14.
161 Ibid vol 2.
162 *Independent Review*, above n 158, 23 (Recommendations No. 15 and 16).
163 UK Government, *UK Government response to the Independent Review of the Modern Slavery Act 2015* (9 July 2019) 7–8 [22] ('*Government response to review*').
164 *Independent Review*, above n 158, 23 (Recommendation No. 19).
165 Ibid 24 (Recommendation No. 21).
166 *Government response to review*, above n 163, 8 [26].
167 Ibid 8 [27].
168 Amending the *Companies Act 2006* (UK) ('*Companies Act*') to include a requirement for companies to refer in their annual reports to their modern slavery

making it a company law offence[169] to fail to report as required, or to fail to act when slavery is found.[170] Businesses should be required to designate a named board member to be personally accountable.[171] The UK Government did not accept the recommendations to amend the *Companies Act*[172] or to create an offence due to concerns that modern slavery statements would become 'high level'.[173] Similarly, the recommendation for an accountable, designated board member was also not supported. Here the UK Government preferred collective responsibility over individual responsibility.[174]

- **Increasing transparency** with a central, government-run repository that is easily accessible to the public, free of charge;[175] clear statements about the requirements on the website repository;[176] and clearly dated statements that specify their reporting period.[177] The UK Government accepted all of these recommendations[178] and further undertook to consult on relevant quality indicators.[179]
- **Monitoring and enforcing compliance**: the Independent Anti-Slavery Commissioner should monitor compliance and the legislation should tackle non-compliance,

> adopting a gradual approach: initial warnings, fines (as a percentage of turnover), court summons and directors' disqualification. Sanctions should be introduced gradually over the next few years so as to give companies time to adapt to changes in the legislative requirements.[180]

---

statement, as well as amending s 54 of the *Modern Slavery Act* to impose a similar duty on non-listed companies that are over the threshold in revenue but are not publicly listed and thus not captured by the *Companies Act* reporting requirements. See *Independent Review*, above n 158, 24 (Recommendation No. 23).

169 Under the *Company Directors Disqualification Act 1986* (UK).
170 *Independent Review*, above n 158, 24 (Recommendation No. 25).
171 Ibid (Recommendation No. 24).
172 *Government response to review*, above n 163, 10 [34].
173 Ibid.
174 Ibid 9 [31].
175 *Independent Review*, above n 158, 24 (Recommendation No. 26).
176 Ibid (Recommendation No. 28).
177 Ibid (Recommendation No. 27).
178 *Government response to review*, above n 163, 10 [32].
179 Home Office, *Transparency in Supply Chains Consultation*, 9 July 2019, 9 ('*Transparency in Supply Chains Consultation*').
180 *Independent Review*, above n 158, 24 (Recommendation No. 30).

- The UK Government should bring forward proposals for an enforcement body, funded by fines levied for non-compliance.[181] In response, the UK Government agreed with the 'gradual approach' stating its concern was 'unintended consequences' such as disincentivising transparency, particularly around modern slavery risks.[182] The UK Government committed to consult with stakeholders. The consultation outlined the UK Government's 'gradual' view in that any non-compliance measure would have a one year minimum lead-in period.[183] The consultation also set out the UK Government's preferred option from the recommendation. That is, a civil penalty proceeding, following non-compliance with a warning letter.[184] The amount would be variable but have a maximum limit and the decision to impose a civil penalty would be subject to appeal.[185] In relation to an enforcement body, the UK Government undertook to consider whether the Home Office or a proposed Single Labour Market Enforcement Body should have responsibility.[186]
- **Government and the public sector**: the reporting requirement should be extended to the public sector and the UK Government should strengthen its public procurement processes.[187] The UK Government agreed with extension of the reporting requirement to the public sector, noting that from 2020 to 2021, ministerial departments would be required to prepare annual statements.[188] To ensure an informed approach, the UK Government undertook to consult on the size and type of public sector organisations that should be covered as well as appropriate approval processes.[189]
- **Consumer attitudes**: the Independent Anti-Slavery Commissioner should commission research on consumer attitudes and the way they can be influenced, so that business, in partnership with civil society, can 'leverage purchasing power to eradicate modern slavery in supply chains'.[190] The Independent Anti-Slavery Commis-

---

181 Ibid (Recommendation No. 31).
182 *Government response to review*, above n 163, 11 [36].
183 *Transparency in Supply Chains Consultation*, above n 179, 9–10.
184 Ibid.
185 Ibid.
186 Ibid.
187 *Independent Review*, above n 158, 24–25 (Recommendation No. 32). See also Recommendations 33–4.
188 *Government response to review*, above n 163, 11 [39].
189 Ibid 12 [40]; *Transparency in Supply Chains Consultation*, above n 179, 12–13.
190 *Independent Review*, above n 158, 25 (Recommendation No. 35).

sioner's annual report should include the research results along with any recommendations for UK Government action. On this matter, the UK Government noted that the Independent Anti-Slavery Commissioner would publish a strategic plan outlining academic research priorities.[191] Further, in July 2019, the UK Government announced the creation of a new modern slavery research centre.

Of these recommendations, the most significant for supply chain transparency and reporting measures were focused on improving the quality of statements in four ways:

- Removing the section that allows entities merely to report 'nil effort' (i.e., that they have taken no steps to address modern slavery in their supply chains).[192] The UK Government in its response acknowledged the need to enhance the reporting criteria and committed to further consulting to ensure appropriate flexibility.[193]
- Changing reporting requirements so that the six areas that an entity's statement 'may' cover would now be mandatory. An entity that decided any of these areas was not applicable to its business should be required to explain why.[194] Here too, the UK Government committed to consulting, seeking to find an appropriate balance between harmonisation with other jurisdictions' reporting requirements and flexibility to 'accommodate the diversity of organisations' subject to the UK legislation.[195]
- Clarification to ensure entities report not merely that they have carried out due diligence but also the steps they intend to take in the future.[196] In response to this recommendation, the UK Government agreed, however, was of the view that this could be achieved without legislative amendment. The UK Government undertook to update the Act's statutory guidance to reflect this recommendation.[197]

---

191 *Government response to review*, above n 163, 12 [44].
192 *Independent Review*, above n 158, 23 (Recommendation No. 17).
193 *Government response to review*, above n 163, 9 [30]; *Transparency in Supply Chains Consultation*, above n 179, 7.
194 *Independent Review*, above n 158, 23 (Recommendation No. 18).
195 *Government response to review*, above n 163, 9 [30]; *Transparency in Supply Chains Consultation*, above n 179, 7.
196 *Independent Review*, above n 158, 24 (Recommendation No. 20).
197 *Government response to review*, above n 163, 9 [29].

- Amending the legislation should be amended so that the entirety of an entity's supply chains is considered. Entities that had not yet done so should be required to explain why, and set out the steps they will take in the future.[198] The UK Government accepted this recommendation, however here too, the view was to achieve this through non-legislative means. Again, the statutory guidance would be updated to set an expectation that 'over time' entities need to extend due diligence along their supply chains, beyond first- and second-tier suppliers.[199]

---

198 *Independent Review*, above n 158, 24 (Recommendation No. 22).
199 *Government response to review*, above n 163, 9 [28].

4 Modern Slavery Act Australia

4.1 Introduction

This chapter details the drafting history of Australia's *Modern Slavery Act 2018*, which passed into law on 10 December 2018, entering into force on 1 January 2019.

In February 2017, the Joint Standing Committee on Foreign Affairs, Defence and Trade ('JSCFADT'),[1] received a referral on the matter from the then Attorney-General, the Hon. George Brandis QC. It in turn referred the inquiry to its Foreign Affairs and Aid Sub-Committee. The terms of reference included consideration of best practices in preventing modern slavery in domestic and global supply chains and whether a Modern Slavery Act should be introduced in Australia.[2]

4.2 The Interim Report: *modern slavery and global supply chains*

It was recognised early on that the UK provisions on transparency in global supply chains (in s 54 of the *Modern Slavery Act 2015*) were '[o]ne of the most significant changes introduced in the Act'[3] and the inquiry proceeded with the UK Act as its primary model. It informed the Interim Report, the Government's MSRR Consultation Paper, and the Final Report.

---

1 The Joint Standing Committee on Foreign Affairs, Defence and Trade ('JSCFADT') for both the Committee and its Subcommittee.
2 Joint Standing Committee on Foreign Affairs, Defence and Trade, Parliament of Australia, *Modern Slavery and Global Supply Chains Interim Report of the Joint Standing Committee on Foreign Affairs, Defence and Trade's Inquiry into Establishing a Modern Slavery Act in Australia* (16 August 2017) ('*the JSCFADT Interim Report*') xi.
3 Joint Standing Committee on Foreign Affairs, Defence and Trade, Parliament of Australia, *Hidden in Plain Sight: An Inquiry into Establishing a Modern Slavery Act in Australia* (December 2017) ('*the Final* Report'), 12 [2.16].

In August 2017, the JSCFADT submitted its Interim Report on the supply chain component of modern slavery, in time for the Bali Process, and clearly with that in mind.[4]

The Interim Report included 'Statements of in-principle support and considerations'.[5] In brief, they were: support for supply chain reporting and support for the UK model, along with proposed principles for Australian legislation.

The Interim Report's three formal recommendations were:[6]

1   In-principle development of a *Modern Slavery Act* in Australia, including 'supply chain reporting requirements for companies, businesses, organisations and governments in Australia, as well as an Independent Anti-Slavery Commissioner, subject to reviewing the recommendations of the JSCFADT's final report.' The recommended content of the Act would be covered in the final report.
2   Treatment of the enactment of a *Modern Slavery Act* in terms of recommendation 1 as 'part of Australia's contribution to the Bali Process reporting requirements'.
3   Treatment of the interim report as part of the Government's

current review of corporate reporting, with a view to developing legislation requiring businesses, companies, organisations and governments operating in Australia to report on measures taken to address modern slavery in their global supply chains, in accordance with the recommendations in the Committee's final report.

In other words, the Interim Report reflected the current thinking that the UK Act was the appropriate model and that enacting it would fulfil current and future obligations. General principles for the Act were

---

4   Australia was hosting the Bali Process Government and Business Forum in Perth on 24 and 25 August 2017, convened jointly by the Foreign Ministers of Indonesia and Australia as an outgrowth of the Sixth Bali Process Ministerial Conference of March 2016. The Bali Process has its own Working Group on Trafficking in Persons (TIP) Forward Work Plan: 2017–19. <https://www.baliprocess.net/UserFiles/baliprocess/File/Bali%20Process%20Trafficking%20in%20Persons%20Working%20Group%20-%20Forward%20Work%20Plan%202017-19%20(002).pdf>.
5   *JSCFADT Interim Report*, above n 2, xvii–xxi.
6   Ibid 56 [4.55]–[4.57].

sketched out,[7] but the substance of the model was left to the Final Report.

In the meantime, submissions were called for and a Parliamentary Delegation to London was organised as part of the inquiry.[8] The delegation included 'meetings with representatives from the UK Government, businesses and NGOs about the development and implementation of the UK *Modern Slavery Act 2015*'.[9]

4.3 The proposed model for public comment

On 16 August 2017, again in time for the Bali Forum to be held in Perth at the end of that month, the Australian Government's proposed model was released in the MSRR Consultation Paper.[10]

In its MSRR Consultation Paper, consistent with its Regulatory Reform Agenda and general approach to deregulation,[11] the Government confined itself to three available options for it to 'support the business community to better respond to modern slavery': do nothing (described as 'business as usual'); encourage business without regulating; and encourage business with minimal regulation (described as 'targeted regulatory action by introducing a Modern Slavery in Supply Chains Reporting Requirement and provide supporting guidance to the business community').

As the Government clearly stated, it was 'not considering other potential options that would impose a high regulatory impact on the business community and may be inconsistent with the Government's Regulatory Reform Agenda'.[12]

The proposed model drew heavily on the UK's *Modern Slavery Act 2015*, with few departures. The most significant departure was a more detailed reporting specification which pinned down the particular

---

7 Ibid xvii–xxi: consistency with international law; a document repository; threshold requirements; prescribing content; guidance for business; penalties for non-compliance; government procurement practice; and an independent Commissioner.
8 Ibid 57–8: the itinerary is set out on pages 57 and 58, and includes attendance at an Asia-Pacific Regional Workshop. The Inquiry received 225 submissions and held 10 public hearings.
9 Ibid 57.
10 Attorney-General's Department (Cth), *Public Consultation Paper and Regulatory Impact Statement for a Modern Slavery in Supply Chains Reporting Requirement* (16 August 2017) ('*MSRR Consultation Paper*').
11 See the *MSRR Consultation Paper*, above n 10, 11.
12 Under the heading 'What Can the Government Do to Address Modern Slavery in Supply Chains?', see *MSRR Consultation Paper*, above n 10, 11–13.

areas on which entities were required to make public disclosures about their due diligence in combating modern slavery.[13]

Having discussed the costs and benefits of the three options it was open to considering, the Government stated its preparedness to accept the cost of the 'minimal regulation' option:[14]

> direct government regulation is appropriate in this context rather than industry self-regulation. This is consistent with the community's expectation that Government will lead on this issue and will ensure that the reporting requirement applies to all appropriate entities and not just specific industries.

While being willing to legislate, the Government noted that its 'preferred option is to develop and implement a Modern Slavery in Supply Chains Reporting Requirement after a period of public consultation'.[15] The rationale was:[16]

> We believe this is on balance the best and most effective way for us to equip and enable the business community to respond effectively to modern slavery and develop and maintain responsible and transparent supply chains. We also believe that the cost of regulating is in proportion to the real-world risk. Modern slavery involves grave abuses of human rights and serous criminal misconduct and it is appropriate that Government takes regulatory action to support the business community to combat this issue.

The legislation the Government was willing to enact was thus framed in terms of facilitation of a structure that would enable business to do the combatting, with a formal reporting structure, but little more.

4.4 The JSCFADT Final Report: committee response to the model

On 7 December 2017, the JSCFADT delivered its response to the Government in its Final Report, titled *Hidden in Plain Sight*. Chapter 5 of that Final Report focuses on transparency in supply chains.

---

13 Discussed in Part 4.5 below.
14 *MSRR Consultation Paper*, above n 10, 13.
15 Ibid 14.
16 Ibid (emphasis added).

66 *Modern Slavery Act Australia*

The JSCFADT framed its response under ten heads, along with recommendations ('R'):

1 Legislative basis (para 5.12);
2 Terminology (paras 5.13–5.23 and R 3, 8);
3 Timeframe for reporting (paras 5.30–5.35 and R 9);
4 Approval of modern slavery statements (paras 5.37–5.38 and R 10);
5 Threshold (paras 5.40–5.48 and R 11);
6 Focus of reporting (paras 5.51–5.63 and R 12);
7 Reporting areas (paras 5.67–5.92, R 13 and R 14);
8 Guidance for business (paras 5.96–5.114 and R 15);
9 Monitoring and evaluation (paras 5.117–5.151, R 16, 17, 18); and
10 Compliance mechanism, oversight (paras 5.152–5.180, R 19).

4.4.1 Where the JSCFADT endorsed the government's proposed model?

In most aspects, the JSCFADT endorsed the Government's proposed model, in some cases with non-substantive differences.

The largely uncontentious matters were set out under six of the ten heads (1, 2, 3, 4, 5, and 7 above). In particular, under (1), the JSCFADT strongly endorsed the Government's approach and recommended 'that this reporting requirement be included in the proposed Modern Slavery Act'.[17]

In relation to *terminology* (2), the JSCFADT referred to its R 3, to the effect that 'the definition of modern slavery should refer to the human trafficking and slavery offences set out in the *Criminal Code*, which are consistent with international law' (at 5.19), but it also thought the definition 'should include reference to child labour and the worst forms of child labour, as well as child exploitation through orphanage trafficking', thus broadening the definition beyond *Criminal Code* offences. Another concern, child exploitation through orphanage tourism was separately addressed in Chapter 8. The definition of 'entity' for reporting purposes was more contentious, as discussed in the following.

In relation to the *timeframe* for reporting (3), submitters had differing views, some seeking phased-in compliance. The JSCFADT (R 9) agreed with the Government's position (five months after the end of the financial year),[18] but with an added option of making a supplementary statement about changed circumstances (at 5.34). It also

---
17 *The Final Report*, above n 3, 95 [5.12].
18 *MSRR Consultation Paper*, above n 10, 15.

proposed a variation relating not to reporting but to penalties (which the Government had not wanted): it recommended a phased introduction of any penalties (at 5.35).

In relation to *approval* (4), the JSCFADT agreed that Board level signoff was appropriate (R 10). On the *threshold* (5) entity size for imposition of the reporting requirement, submissions varied quite widely. The Government proposed a monetary measure of annual revenue of at least $100 million, with an opt-in option for smaller entities, and no consideration of industry-based risk.[19] In R 11, after discussion of the various views of submitters, the Committee endorse the Government's proposal in general, but reduced the threshold revenue figure to $50 million.

In the matter of *reporting areas* (7), the model had departed from the UK precedent in proposing fixed criteria against which entities would have to report. While some submitters opposed fixed criteria, others believed them to provide better certainty than was available under the UK model. The Committee supported the more prescriptive approach; it also recommended that an entity could supply its statement in satisfaction of requests for information (R 13). In other words, entities should not be subjected to the burden of supplying multiple, variably worded sets of information to other requesting entities doing their own due diligence (at 5.76). After extensive discussion of the submissions, practices of other countries in relation to due diligence and its burdens, the JSCFADT set out R 14, 'which takes in account the outcomes of the Australian Government's consultation process, best practice in international jurisdictions and the suggested areas outlined in section 54(5) of the UK *Modern Slavery Act 2015*' (at 5.93). These areas relate to the entity's structure, business and supply chains; its modern slavery policies; its due diligence and remediation processes; its areas of risk and risk-assessment steps taken; outcomes measures of effectiveness; training; and other action taken to eradicate modern slavery. In addition, the JSCFADT recommended considering other measures, such as mandatory due diligence, as part of a three-year legislative review (R 14).

This was all largely consonant with the Government view, apart from an additional reporting area for 'other action' and enabling smaller entities to use their statements to satisfy other entities that they had found no modern slavery in their own supply chains after due diligence.

19 Ibid.

In relation to *monitoring and evaluation* (9), the Government uncontentiously proposed a central, publicly searchable repository for reports as well as publication on modern slavery statements on entities' websites, and the JSCFADT supported this approach (R 16, 17). A minor extension was that an entity without website could publish the statement in its annual report or other public document. It also recommended that the Government provide details of entities that were required to report along with their compliance, and particulars of entities below the threshold which were voluntarily reporting (R 18).

The Government proposed a *compliance mechanism* (10) including 'considering options for oversight of the reporting requirement, including the feasibility of and requirement for independent oversight', without specifically designating the role of a Commissioner. Any oversight mechanism implemented 'could perform a number of functions, including: maintaining the central repository of statements, raising awareness about modern slavery risks, and/or providing a single point of contact for businesses seeking advice and assistance'.[20] The JSCFADT recommended an Anti-Slavery Commissioner position for this role (at 5.180).

The Government was also 'considering ways to support business groups and civil society to undertake analysis and benchmarking of Modern Slavery Statements'. It would 'assess compliance with the reporting requirement during the proposed post-implementation review of the legislation after three years'.[21] The JSCFADT supported this approach.

4.4.2 Points on which the final report differs from the government's position

The JSCFADT departed from the model with more significant differences. These were matters 2, 6, 8, 9, 10, each discussed briefly below. However, the general picture is of JSCFADT endorsement of the Government's model as presented in the MSRR Consultation Paper of August 2017.

Although, under heading (2), *Terminology*, the JSCFADT largely agreed with the Government on the definition of modern slavery (albeit expanding it beyond the *Criminal Code* offences), it disagreed more significantly on the definition of 'entities' to be affected. It broadened this category to include more than 'bodies corporate, unincorporated

---

20 Ibid 17.
21 Ibid.

associations or bodies of persons, superannuation funds and approved deposit funds'.[22] Its own definition was more generally defined to cover 'companies, businesses, organisations, governments and other bodies' (at 5.22). Thus, R 8 was framed non-restrictively to 'include, but not be limited to, companies; businesses; organisations (including religious bodies); Commonwealth government agencies and public bodies; the Australian Government; bodies corporate; unincorporated associations or bodies of persons; sole traders; partnerships; trusts; superannuation funds; and approved deposit funds'.

This meant, as the JSCFADT recommended, that the Government comply with the reporting requirement itself.[23] Preferring various submitters' views on this point, the JSCFADT agreed that the Government should set a positive example by procuring goods and services only from compliant companies. To that end, it proposed an opt-in provision that would enable smaller organisations (below the proposed threshold) to opt in if they wanted to obtain government contracts.[24]

The issue of Government compliance arises again under *Focus of reporting* (6). The discussion on the reporting focus is brief (a single paragraph repeating the Government's view):[25]

> all entities headquartered in Australia, or entities that have any part of their operations in Australia, and meet the revenue threshold' be required to 'report on their actions to address modern slavery in both their *operations* and their *supply chains*.

The remainder of the *Focus* topic is set out under the subheadings 'Entities required to report' and 'Public procurement', at which point the Report enters an extended discussion culminating in its view (at 5.63) that 'governments and public bodies above the reporting threshold size be required to report to demonstrate the steps they have taken to address modern slavery risks in their operations and supply chains'. R 12 is framed accordingly, to apply to all entities operating in Australia, regardless of where they are headquartered, reporting on both their operations and their supply chains (at 5.51 and 5.52).

---

22 Submission 89 to the JSCFADT Inquiry into establishing a Modern Slavery Act in Australia, April 2017, 15.
23 *Final Report*, above n 3, 105–7.
24 Ibid 101 [5.41].
25 Ibid 10 [5.51], citing the *MSRR Consultation Paper*, above n 10, 15.

Under *guidance for business* (8), the Government's proposal was relatively modest. The Committee noted that the Government:[26]

> proposed to provide 'clear and detailed guidance and awareness-raising materials for the business community', which could include: ... a reporting template, best-practice examples and information about how the business community can remedy and report instances of modern slavery identified in their supply chains or operations.'

The JSCFADT expanded on this modest government contribution with a much more comprehensive idea of support – including advice, awareness raising and training, which 'includes training for companies, businesses, front-line services, government departments and embassies' (at 5.103) – and it referred back to the view it had set out in the Interim Report that training was critical.[27] 'Detailed, clear guidance' about expectations should be prepared in consultation with the proposed Independent Anti-Slavery Commissioner (R 15).

In addition, the Government should define 'supply chain' in a manner 'consistent with the OECD Due Diligence Guidance' (at 5.109)[28] as well as publishing a list of at-risk industries, products, areas and people, as submitters had requested (at 5.110).

In relation to *monitoring and evaluation* (9), while some recommendations made by the Government were supported by the JSCFADT (as noted above), more contentiously, the Government preferred, as in the UK, not to include punitive penalties for noncompliance.[29] The weight of public opprobrium was argued to be sufficient: '[t]The Australian Government will monitor general compliance with the reporting requirement and entities that do not comply with the reporting requirement may be subject to public criticism.'

---

26 *MSRR Consultation Paper*, above n 10, 16 [5.6].
27 *JSCFADT Interim Report*, above n 2, 52.
28 *MSSR Consultation Paper*, above n 10, 10: the definitions vary; the Government had indicated its support for extending the reporting requirement beyond tier 1 suppliers by 'encouraging the business community to identify and address modern slavery risks beyond first tier suppliers and through their entire supply chains'.
29 Ibid 17.

In relation to *compliance measures* (10), after discussing the varying views of submitters at some length, the Committee supported the perspective put by business 'that introducing compliance measures and penalties for identifying and addressing modern slavery risks would discourage businesses from reporting, or being open in their reporting' and therefore 'does not support penalties or compliance measures for companies that identify and report on steps taken to address modern slavery risks' (at 5.165–6). It nevertheless recommended that there should be 'penalties and compliance measures for entities that fail to report' (R 19). However, there should be wide consultation and phasing-in of such measures. ASIC was conceived as 'a possible role' (at 5.172).

4.5 Modern Slavery Bill 2018

Consistent with the general approach, the JSCFADT's views, as expressed in its Final Report and recommendations, were largely incorporated in the Australian Government's Modern Slavery Bill, with two notable exceptions: the revenue threshold at which compliance became mandatory, and the penalties for non-compliance.

4.5.1 The general shape of the Bill

Businesses operating within the Australian market (whether locally based or merely trading in Australia) would be required to report annually if their consolidated revenue exceeds $100 million. Reporting covers perceived risks and actions in response. Beyond the mandatory regime, the Bill provided for voluntary reporting by other entities based or operating in Australia.[30]

Rather than focusing purely on corporate commercial entities in the market, the Bill also required the Commonwealth to report on behalf of its non-corporate agencies (Commonwealth corporate entities to report themselves), again based on a revenue threshold of $100 million.[31]

The Bill provided for free public access to the information filed under the reporting regime. The Minister was to keep statements in a public repository accessible on the Internet. This unrestricted-access repository would be called the Modern Slavery Statements Register.[32]

---

30 Modern Slavery Bill 2018 (Cth) Part 1 ('*Modern Slavery Bill*').
31 Ibid.
32 Ibid.

4.5.2 The modern slavery statement

Under the terms of the Bill, an annual modern slavery statement was to be submitted to the Minister by each reporting entity, covering the entity itself, along with other entities it owned or controlled. The statement was required to describe the risks of modern slavery occurring in the entity's operations and supply chains and set out the actions being taken to address them.[33]

Joint modern slavery statements were permissible on behalf of one or more reporting entities.[34]

The Minister was required to prepare annual statements for non-corporate Commonwealth entities that were required to file them.[35]

All reporting entities, government or non-government, must address certain matters in their statements. The mandatory compliance criteria supplied a consistent structure across statements, and this approach was intended to clarify the obligations of reporting entities, for their own compliance focus, as well as enabling cross-comparisons between entities.[36]

Each report was to set out the identity of the reporting entity (along with its structure, operations and supply chains) and describe the way it was addressing each of the other mandatory criteria, for its own operations and supply chains and for the operations and supply chains of its subsidiary entities (i.e., those it owned or controlled):

- the modern slavery risks;
- the actions taken to address those risks, including due diligence and remediation processes;
- how the effectiveness of those actions is assessed;
- what consultation with subsidiary entities was carried out to prepare the statement; and
- any other relevant information.[37]

Where joint statements were filed, they must address each of these criteria for each entity that is party to the statement. Again, each reporting entity covered by the joint statement was to be identified (along with its structure, operations, and supply chains) and the

---

33 Ibid Part 2.
34 Ibid.
35 Ibid.
36 Explanatory Memorandum, Modern Slavery Bill 2018 (Cth) [119].
37 Ibid [120].

statement must describe the way each was addressing the mandatory criteria, for its own operations and supply chains and for the operations and supply chains of subsidiary entities. The same structure applied for the operations and supply chains of each constituent entity in the joint statement and its subsidiaries: its risk, actions, assessment of effectiveness, consultations, and any other relevant information.[38]

4.5.3 The modern slavery register

The Bill established the Modern Slavery Statements Register at the core of the reporting regime. The Minister (through departmental delegates) received statements and made them available to the public on the Internet. The Bill also allowed for filing of revised versions of registered statements.[39]

The Minister must establish and maintain the Register as a freely accessible, and free, public website repository of registered statements. The Register was to function transparently, contributing to the effectiveness of reporting requirements by ensuring that statements were readily identified and easily accessed by the public. Entities could also make copies of their filed statements available elsewhere, for example on their own websites.[40]

Ministerial discretion included not registering a statement that did not meet the mandatory criteria. Thus, for example, where there had been serious noncompliance with the regime, the Minister could decline to register a statement.[41]

The nature of the Minister's decision-making power meant that an exercise of the discretion not to register was not subject to formal external review on the merits. Consistent with the scope of the administrative power, it was intended that an exercise of the discretion would occur in very limited circumstances of 'egregious noncompliance'. Such a decision would not be made unless reasonable attempts to discuss compliance and assist the affected entity to comply with the minimum legislated criteria in its statement.[42]

---

38 Ibid [124].
39 *Modern Slavery Bill*, Part 3.
40 Explanatory Memorandum, Modern Slavery Bill 2018 (Cth) [135].
41 Ibid [138].
42 Ibid [147].

4.6 Parliamentary Joint Committee on Human Rights report

In its human rights scrutiny report,[43] the Parliamentary Joint Committee on Human Rights focused on the compatibility of the regime with multiple rights, in particular the right to privacy, which the Committee was concerned might be restricted by the operation of the legislation.

The Committee acknowledged the positive nature of the Bill, and approved it from a human rights perspective. It found the reporting requirements a welcome measure that promoted the right to freedom from slavery and forced labour.[44]

Turning to privacy and the need to protect it, the Committee was less sanguine. Noting that the right 'encompasses respect for informational privacy, including the right to respect for private information and private life, particularly the storing, use and disclosure of personal information',[45] the Committee observed that the Modern Slavery Statements which entities were required to lodge would be published online, and while the information they contained was generally business-related rather than focusing on individuals, in some cases the interconnections may be such as to render 'business' information personal; in addition, there was what it called a 'very small' risk of a statement directly identifying victims or potential victims.[46] In those situations, privacy would be compromised and rights curtailed, to the detriment of individuals, including potential exposure to greater risk than before.[47]

While the Government's statement of compatibility recognised that the legislation does intersect with privacy rights in a way that limits those rights, the Government found that 'reasonable and necessary' to meet the objectives of the Bill (strengthening Australia's approach to modern slavery).[48] The Committee conceded that the objective was likely to be legitimate (i.e., within the Commonwealth's power to enact), and that the proposed reporting regime was rationally connected to that objective.[49] In addition, it agreed with the Government that the protective

---

43 Parliamentary Joint Committee on Human Rights, Parliament of Australia, *Human Rights Scrutiny Report, No. 8 of 2018* (2018).
44 Ibid 20 [1.69]–[1.70].
45 Ibid 20 [1.71], with further reference to Appendix 2.
46 Ibid 20–1 [1.72].
47 Ibid 21 [1.73].
48 Ibid 21 [1.74]–[1.75].
49 Ibid 21 [1.75].

measures in place[50] did offer safeguards that were 'important and relevant to the proportionality of the measures'.[51]

The measures included regulated collection and retention of information; limited disclosure requirements; detailed guidance that stressed the importance of privacy; publicly accessible legislation and guidance; collection only by the Minister and delegates; and collection only of prescribed information. However, despite being 'important and relevant', what was absent was any statutory prohibition on including personal or identifying information,[52] or on the Minister disclosing such information.[53]

Having concluded that privacy remained at risk, the Committee sought clarification from the Minister on safeguards to protect the privacy of victims or potential victims.[54]

4.7 Senate Legal and Constitutional Affairs Legislation Committee Report

On 28 June 2018, the Senate Legal and Constitutional Affairs Legislation Committee received a reference to conduct an inquiry on the Modern Slavery Bill. The Senate Committee called for submissions by 20 July 2018, and 93 were received. It then conducted three public hearings in early August,[55] and reported to the Parliament on 24 August 2018.

4.7.1 *The revenue threshold*

There were five broad themes or arguments, four of which pointed to some other, more appropriate measure.

The first three, arguing for a lower threshold, were: that an $100 million threshold would capture too few organisations;[56] that a lower threshold of $25 million would align the new measures with existing regulatory requirements for large proprietary companies, defined at

---

50 Ibid 21–2 [1.76].
51 Ibid 22 [1.77].
52 Ibid.
53 Ibid 22 [1.78].
54 Ibid 22 [1.79]–[1.80].
55 The hearings took place in Melbourne on 1 August 2018, in Sydney on 2 August 2018, and in Canberra on 3 August 2018: Senate Legal and Constitutional Affairs Legislation Committee, *Modern Slavery Bill 2018 [Provisions]*, 24 August 2018, 15 [2.31] ('*Bill Provisions 2018*').
56 Ibid 28 [3.36].

that threshold in s 45A *Corporations Act 2001* (Cth);[57] and that a lower threshold of $50 million would better align with the NSW framework ($50 million) and the UK threshold of £36 million (approximately $60 million).[58] The fourth view accepted the Bill's draft threshold on the basis that reducing the threshold below $100 million would impose too great a regulatory burden.[59]

A fifth suggestion was to depart from the 'threshold' approach and instead take a targeted, 'risk-based approach' to reporting. Doing so would enable high-risk industries to be identified and entities operating within those industries to be required to report, without revenue-based exclusions.

The Senate Committee itself ultimately supported the Bill's $100 million threshold as, on balance, the best approach. It considered the initial pool of 3,000 entities a substantial enough component of the commercial world to drive reform across industries within their own supply chains, which would bring smaller entities within the scope of the reforms without increasing their regulatory burden to any great extent.[60] It noted the proposed three-year review to reconsider or fine-tune the regime, or even to adopt a risk-based approach.[61]

On this basis, the Senate Committee recommended that the statutory three-year review be used to consider all aspects of the Act, with particular attention to compliance thresholds.[62]

4.7.2 Penalties

Those making submissions and giving evidence in favour advocated penalties for failure to prepare the required statement or preparing incomplete, deceptive, misleading or fraudulent statements.[63] Without such penalties, it was argued, compliance rates would be low, being in effect voluntary and merely industry-driven.[64]

Those against penalties promoted the virtue of being consistent with the established legislative regimes in the UK and California;[65] supported organisation-driven, rather than compliance-driven responses,

---

57 Ibid.
58 Ibid 28 [3.37].
59 Ibid 29 [3.42]–[3.43].
60 Ibid 39 [3.83].
61 Ibid 39 [3.84].
62 Ibid 41 [3.100] (Recommendation No. 4).
63 Ibid 25 [3.26].
64 Ibid 25 [3.27].
65 Ibid 23 [3.20].

since those were, they argued, more likely to lead to lasting and meaningful changes in businesses;[66] preferred to take a corporate-cultural route that would embed a culture of positive change to corporate behaviour through encouragement;[67] and foster a 'race to the top' in competitive corporate culture.[68]

It was also argued whether or not penalties applied in the establishment phase (the first three years), the question of penalties should be revisited as part of the three-year review.[69]

Those who argued in favour of penalties made a range of proposals: high financial penalties commensurate with those in the NSW regime (up to $1.1 million, i.e., 1,000 penalty units, as a criminal sanction), which would standardise sanctions across (NSW) state and Commonwealth regimes; smaller sanctions under a civil penalty regime that would, it was argued, operate as a form of shaming by publicly signalling the entity's non-compliance.

Specific suggestions about various aspects of sanctions were made: imposing criminal penalties not just on the entities themselves, but on their directors or other senior executives; imposing harsher penalties for repeat offences; placing barriers to market participation by non-compliant entities, in the form of rendering non-compliant entities ineligible to tender for Commonwealth contracts, receive grants, or obtain trade or consular assistance; introducing 'shaming' measures for consistently bad behaviour in the form of naming in Parliament or public listing on a register of non-compliant bodies.[70]

It was also suggested that a penalty regime might be introduced progressively, being phased in over the first 12 months of operation of the Act.[71]

While not being opposed to penalties in principle, the Senate Committee took the view that it would be better to have the advantage of the compliance data that would be available after the first three years before imposing a penalty scheme. After the three-year review, the scope and potential effectiveness of a penalty scheme would be more apparent, since more would be known at that point about the Act's operation and compliance with it.[72]

---

66 Ibid.
67 Ibid.
68 Ibid.
69 Ibid 27 [3.32].
70 Ibid 26 [3.30].
71 Ibid 27 [3.31].
72 Ibid 39 [3.81].

On this basis, the Senate Committee again recommended that the statutory three-year review be used to reconsider penalties, whether that might be a mandatory penalty regime or a finding that penalties were evidently not needed.[73]

4.7.3 Public list of entities

In relation to a public register of entities required to comply, those in favour argued that the Bill should include a provision requiring Government to develop and publish such a list,[74] and that liability to comply could be determined by referring to the annually published Australian Tax Office's (ATO) Corporate Tax Transparency Report (CTTR).[75]

The Department of Home Affairs argued against such a list, stressing the difficulties that could be expected in both establishing it and maintaining it, which would be resource-intensive. It pointed out that the ATO's CTTR was inadequate, by itself, for the purpose; corporate group structures, the absence of foreign income entities and non-tax-consolidated groups complicated the picture from an ATO data perspective, so not all relevant reporting entities would be captured.[76] The Department also noted that fluctuating revenues and changing corporate structures build risk into the process. This meant there was potential to incorrectly identify entities, potentially damaging their reputation and finances.[77]

In its formal recommendation on this issue, the Senate Committee recommended the Government work towards establishing a list of 'reporting entities' and publishing compliance standards. This would test motivational power of reputational risk for reporting entities.[78] The positive arm was to publicly list entities that do comply.[79]

4.7.4 Anti-Slavery Commissioner

The Senate Committee noted the support, from several quarters, for the appointment of an independent statutory anti-slavery officer.[80] It summarised the arguments for and against such an appointment,[81]

---

73 Ibid 41 [3.100] (Recommendation No. 4).
74 Ibid 33 [3.54].
75 Ibid 33 [3.55].
76 Ibid 34 [3.57].
77 Ibid 34 [3.58].
78 Ibid 41 [3.97] (Recommendation No. 1).
79 Ibid 41 [3.98] (Recommendation No. 2).
80 Ibid 17–18 [3.3].
81 Ibid 17–23 [3.3]–[3.18].

stated that it endorsed the view that a Commissioner was needed,[82] and made a formal recommendation accordingly.[83]

Citing resourcing issues, the Government pressed for an internal Business Engagement Unit, which it said would be better placed to perform all necessary functions.[84] In any case, the question could be revisited as part of the three-year review.[85]

4.8 Government response to Senate Legal and Constitutional Affairs Legislation Committee report

The Government responded to the Senate Committee report in October 2018.[86]

4.8.1 The revenue threshold

The Senate Committee recommended:[87]

> that the statutory three-year review consider all aspects of the Act, *with particular attention to compliance thresholds and compliance standards*, and that the review be required to consider whether a mandatory penalty regime is required, drawing on the evidence and data gathered through the first three years of the Act's operation. The committee acknowledges that it may be shown that penalties are not needed.
>
> (Emphasis added)

In its response, the Government accepted the recommendation.[88] However, it did not directly address the threshold issue, either in its response or in the suite of eight amendments to make to the Bill.

4.8.2 Penalties

In accepting Recommendation 4,[89] the Government said it would 'clarify the focus' of the review and provide a 'clear pathway' for the

---

82 Ibid 38 [3.79].
83 Ibid 41 [3.99] (Recommendation No. 3).
84 Ibid 22 [3.17].
85 Ibid 23 [3.18].
86 Australian Government, *Australian Government Response to the Senate Legal and Constitutional Affairs Legislation Committee Report on the Modern Slavery Bill 2018* (2018) ('the Government's Response').
87 *Bill Provisions 2018*, above n 55, 41 [3.100].
88 *The Government's Response*, above n 86 [3.100].
89 Ibid.

introduction of penalties if compliance rates proved to be inadequate without them.

4.8.3 Public list of entities

The Senate Committee's Recommendations 1 and 2 worked together to 'test the proposition that "reputational risk" is a sufficient motivator for reporting entities to comply with the requirements of the Act'.[90] To this end, Recommendation 1 was to 'work towards building a list of "reporting entities", and to publish compliance standards publicly', and Recommendation 2 was to publish lists of those who did report (as required, or voluntarily).

The Government's response was to accept the first 'in principle', and to accept the second more enthusiastically, without demur. Indeed, it 'recognise[d] the importance' of public accessibility of information and described the legislation as a 'world-first initiative' that would provide 'an easily accessible, public mechanism to identify all entities' that had reported. And it would consider 'other options to publish lists' such as ministerial reports to Parliament.[91] Here, it referred to its response to Recommendation 4, where it accepted that the Minister should be required to report to Parliament.

The Government's concern about Recommendation 1 was that it had determined 'that it is not possible to publish a complete and verifiable public list' because of data limitations and other practical difficulties, as well as the possibility of exposing entities to reputational risk, should the public register prove incorrect.[92]

4.8.4 Anti-Slavery Commissioner

Although the Senate Committee recommended[93] that an independent statutory officer be appointed, the Government merely noted the recommendation and reiterated its view[94] that an internal Business Unit within the Department of Home affairs would not only suffice, but be 'the best body to support the operation of the reporting requirement'.[95]

---

90 *Bill Provisions 2018*, above n 55, 41 [3.97]–[3.98] (Recommendations No. 1 and 2).
91 *The Government's Response*, above n 86 [3.98].
92 Ibid 56 [3.97].
93 *Bill Provisions 2018*, above n 55, 41 [3.99] (Recommendation No. 3).
94 *The Government's Response*, above n 86 [3.99].
95 Ibid.

4.9 Minister's response to Parliamentary Joint Committee on Human Rights information request

The Assistant Minister, Senator Linda Reynolds, delivered the Minister's Response to the proposed legislation.

While the Committee had been concerned about privacy, the Government took the view that in general, the risk that the legislation would result in privacy breaches through disclosure of personal information was low. The Ministerial response was therefore 'that the safeguards contained in the Bill are ... sufficient in light of that low risk' and that a careful assessment of other approaches led to the conclusion that they would not be any more effective than detailed guidance that contained case studies and comprehensive advice. Other possible approaches included amending the Bill to expressly provide that statements are not to include personal or identifying information.[96]

Having reconsidered its assessment in light of the response, the Committee[97] conceded that the Minister's position might be correct – that privacy was not seriously at risk under the regime as presently conceived – but that knowing how the legislation operated in practice was necessary. It therefore recommended monitoring of the privacy aspects of the regime (in terms of the implementation of the legislation generally, including compliance with the guidance issued) to ensure that the Minister's assessment of the situation turned out, in fact, to be the case.[98]

Given the central role being played by guidance materials in this regime, the Committee, not surprisingly, requested that any such material be supplied to it when available.[99]

4.10 Bill's Second Reading debate – House of Representatives

The Bill returned for its Second Reading and consideration by the 45th Parliament in September 2018.[100] During debate on 12 and 17 September, 30 MPs spoke to the Bill in the House of Representatives.

---

96 Parliamentary Joint Committee on Human Rights, Parliament of Australia, *Human Rights Scrutiny Report No. 11* (2018) 102 [2.97] (*'Human Rights Scrutiny Report No. 11'*).
97 Through its Chair, Mr Ian Goodenough MP.
98 *Human Rights Scrutiny Report No. 11*, above n 96, 103 [2.102].
99 Ibid 104 [2.103].
100 Alex Hawke MP, Assistant Minister for Home Affairs, had presented the Bill to the House with a Second Reading Speech on 28 June 2018, after which the debate was adjourned. He expressed the Government's desire for speedy passage of the

The Australian Labor Party, with by far the majority of speakers to the Bill,[101] moved amendments in two main areas (the inclusion of a penalty regime and an independent Anti-Slavery Commissioner) and two other, less critical, areas.[102] Ms O'Neil stressed that while Labor took a bipartisan approach, it was concerned about unintended consequences. Sharon Claydon MP agreed the Bill was 'an important first step; it's just not going far enough'.[103] All proposed amendments were ultimately defeated in votes along party lines,[104] but the Second Reading speeches pinpoint potential future issues.

The first proposed amendment of substance was the penalty regime. In the form presented to the House at the Second Reading stage, it took the form of a civil penalty (1,000 penalty units) for failure to prepare or give a modern slavery statement.[105] Machinery provisions included enforcement of civil penalties,[106] for which the Secretary of the Department would be authorised to apply[107] to a court with federal jurisdiction.[108] The Crown would be excluded from the penalty regime.[109]

The driving force was to give the legislation real teeth.[110] As Ms Aly noted in her speech, '[t]he Law Council [of Australia] considers that without penalties, a mandatory reporting requirement is ren-

---

legislation, saying, 'I look forward to working with those opposite and those in the other place, to ensure that this bill is passed before the end of the year:' Commonwealth, *Parliamentary Debates*, House of Representatives, 28 June 2018, 6758.

101 A total of 22 Labor Party MPs. In addition, Adam Bandt (Greens) spoke, along with seven Liberals (Andrew Hasties; David Coleman; Chris Crewther; Luke Howarth; Ted O'Brien; Keith Pitt; Tim Wilson, in addition to Alex Hawke's First Reading speech on 28 June 2018. The Country Nationals Senator Nigel Scullion spoke to the Bill on 18 September 2018 as it was adjourned to the next sitting.
102 Proposed by Clare O'Neil.
103 Commonwealth, *Parliamentary Debates*, House of Representatives, 12 September 2018, 8765 (Sharon Claydon).
104 Ibid 8736–69.
105 *Modern Slavery Bill*, proposed amendments, s 16A (Clare O'Neil).
106 Under the *Regulatory Powers (Standard Provisions) Act 2014* (Cth) Part 4, proposed s 22A(1).
107 Proposed s 22A(2).
108 The Federal Court of Australia, Federal Circuit Court of Australia, or a court of a State or Territory that has jurisdictions in relation to the matter: proposed s 22A(3); the provisions would extend to 'every external Territory and acts, omissions, matters and things outside Australia': proposed s 22A(4).
109 Proposed s 22A(5).
110 The 'toothless' tiger metaphor was variously invoked in the Second Reading speeches of Labor members Graham Perrett, Tanya Plibersek, Chris Hayes, Tim Watts, and Mark Dreyfus.

dered merely aspirational'. While consumer-facing entities are sensitive to reputational risk, she added, that 'does not apply equally to all entities'.[111] Milton Dick quoted Keren Adams, a Director of Legal Advocacy at the Australian Human Rights Law Centre, on the point: 'A mandatory reporting scheme is not really mandatory if there are no consequences for companies that fail to comply.'[112]

Ms O'Neil argued that the lesson from the UK was that penalties were needed.[113] Gai Brodtmann expressed disappointment with the supposedly bipartisan process, again saying that evidence from the UK had been ignored.[114] Ms Kearney also cited the UK experience, saying:

> there were no penalties, [and] the percentage of businesses that have reported still hovers around 30 per cent of those who have an obligation to do so. I'm sorry, but that is not good enough.[115]

Another Labor member, Steve Georganas, made the same point even more forcefully.[116] Labor members were thus unified in the matter of penalties.

The contrary (Government) position was to allow market forces to exert pressure rather than over-regulating, as earlier noted by Alex Hawke, Assistant Minister for Home Affairs, with his 'race to the top' metaphor:[117]

> Critically, it will also drive a 'race to the top' as reporting entities compete for market funding and investor and consumer support.
>
> Businesses that fail to take action will be penalised by the market and consumers and severely tarnish their reputations.

This position was restated by Ted O'Brien, MP (Liberal).[118]

---

111 Commonwealth, *Parliamentary Debates*, House of Representatives, 12 September 2018, 8828.
112 Ibid 8842.
113 Ibid 8739–40.
114 Ibid 8848.
115 Ibid 8823.
116 Ibid 8834.
117 Commonwealth, *Parliamentary Debates*, House of Representatives 28 June 2018, 6755 (Alex Hawke).
118 Commonwealth, *Parliamentary Debates*, House of Representatives, 12 September 2018, 8753 (Ted O'Brien).

The upshot was that those who spoke in favour of the amendment (all Labor) were numerous.[119] Only one member spoke against the amendment (Mr O'Brien, Liberal).

The second proposed amendment of major import was to establish the office of independent Anti-Slavery Commissioner in place of a Business Engagement Unit within the Department. Pressing this point, Labor noted its commitment to establish an independent office if it gained power.[120] Greens representative Adam Bandt also spoke in support of this proposal:[121]

> just as we needed laws that held large companies like Nike and Adidas to account and enabled them to be taken to court, we need laws in this country that have teeth. To pass modern slavery legislation but then outsource effective compliance of that to the very same people that this is meant to be regulating raises the question about whether the bill is going to work at all....

Ms Brodtmann, as one of 21 members whose Second Reading speeches supported the proposed amendment, noted that 'key stakeholders, including ACRATH, Anti-Slavery Australia and the ACTU have joined Labor in the call for the establishment of an Independent Anti-Slavery Commissioner' and added that Labor would 'be fighting to ensure that Australia gets a Slavery Act that will actually make a difference'.[122]

Others speaking in support argued that, as an independent body, a Commission would oversee the Act, receive complaints, and support victims,[123] as well as helping businesses achieve best practice in their supply chains.[124]

---

119 Graham Perrett, Matt Thistlethwaite, Tanya Plibersek, Clare O'Neil, Chris Hayes, Tim Watts, Julian Hill, Sharon Claydon, Ross Hart, Ged Kearney, Mark Dreyfus, Anne Aly, Steve Georganas, Andrew Leigh, Peter Khalil, Milton Dick, Gai Brodtmann, Josh Wilson, Graham Perret, Lisa Chesters, Tony Zappia and Matt Keogh.

120 Commonwealth, *Parliamentary Debates*, House of Representatives, 12 September 2018, 8741 (Clare O'Neil).

121 Commonwealth, *Parliamentary Debates*, House of Representatives, 17 September 2018, 9151 (Adam Bandt).

122 Commonwealth, *Parliamentary Debates*, House of Representatives, 12 September 2018, 8821 (Gai Brodtmann).

123 Members supporting this argument in their speeches (all Labor): Tanya Plibersek, Clare O'Neil, Tim Watts, Sharon Claydon, Ross Hart, Ged Kearney, Mark Dreyfus, Matt Keogh, Steve Georganas, Peter Khalil, Dick Milton, Josh Wilson and Lisa Chesters.

124 Minister supporting this argument in their speeches: Tanya Plibersek, Adam Bandt, Tim Watts, Ross Hart, Mark Dreyfus, Anne Aly, and Peter Khalil.

The Government stance, on the other hand, was to save costs and avoid fragmenting anti-slavery efforts across different bodies; in particular, an existing Human Rights Commission structure was already in place to do this work. This point of view was defended by a former Human Rights Commissioner, Tim Wilson, who saw it as the pragmatic solution.[125]

A third proposed amendment was to remove forced marriage from the definition of modern slavery.[126] This change was sought over concern its inclusion could potentially drive the practice further underground.[127]

Six Labor MPs supported the proposal and spoke on the point.[128] Tanya Plibersek explained Labor's reasoning, based on advice from advocates working in the field.[129] Noting that the current approach, relying on the *Criminal Code*, had not yielded any prosecutions for forced marriage, and that alternative protections under the civil law was limited – as was Government financial support – Plibersek stressed that the ALP's approach, as set out in current policy, was to establish a separate, and separately funded, forced marriage protection regime comprising orders, agency support and a one-stop 'forced marriage' unit to connect victims to support services.

A fourth proposed amendment was to require the Minister to report to Parliament annually on compliance by reporting entities, listing entities that failed to report.[130]

In the end, as noted, voting on party lines led to defeat of all proposed amendments in the House.[131]

---

125 Commonwealth, *Parliamentary Debates*, House of Representatives, 12 September 2018, 8758 (Tim Wilson).
126 Commonwealth, *Parliamentary Debates*, House of Representatives, 17 September 2018, 9158; *Modern Slavery Bill* 2018, Proposed Amendments (Clare O'Neil).
127 Shadow Ministers and Ministers supporting this argument: Tanya Plibersek, Clare O'Neil, Tim Watts and Mark Dreyfus.
128 Commonwealth, *Parliamentary Debates*, House of Representatives, 12 September 2018, 8741–2 (Clare O'Neil), 8756 (Tim Watts), 8826–7 (Mark Dreyfus), 8832 (Matt Keogh), 8840 (Matt Keogh); 9154–5 (Tanya Plibersek).
129 Commonwealth, *Parliamentary Debates*, House of Representatives, 17 September 2018, 9152–5 (Tanya Plibersek).
130 *Modern Slavery Bill 2018*, Proposed Amendments, proposed s 16B (Clare O'Neil).
131 Commonwealth, *Parliamentary Debates*, House of Representatives, 17 September 2018, 1824–5: In each case (penalties; Ministerial reporting requirement; and removal of forced marriage from the regime): 67 Yes, 72 No. In the case of Anti-Slavery Commissioner – 68 Yes, 72 No.

4.11 Senate consideration

After the First Reading speech, the Bill had been referred to the Senate Legal and Constitutional Affairs Legislation Committee, and the Committee's report, dated 24 August 2018, included recommended amendments.[132] Accordingly, when the Bill moved into the Senate on 18 September 2018, the Government moved three amendments, with the stated purpose of improving the operation of the Bill by:[133]

> [e]stablishing an appropriate mechanism to address noncompliance; strengthening Parliamentary oversight of the implementation of the Modern Slavery Reporting Requirement; and providing a clear pathway to future civil penalties if initial compliance rates are inadequate.

Senator Nigel Scullion, Minister for Indigenous Affairs and Leader of The Nationals in the Senate gave the Government's Second Reading speech.[134]

The first amendment proposed in the Senate, establishing an appropriate mechanism to address noncompliance, was a new Section 16A that did not, as Labor had wanted, include penalties. However, it established a mechanism by which non-compliant entities could be dealt with in the first three years of implementation.

The cornerstone of the proposed mechanism was a 'please explain' power by which the Minister may request an entity to explain its non-compliance, or to take remedial action. The Minister would need to be reasonably satisfied that the entity was in fact non-compliant, but that could mean any of the requirements under the Act not being met.[135]

The examples of remedial action that would be open to the Minister to take were: 'a requirement to give a Modern Slavery Statement to the Minister' and revising a Modern Slavery Statement.[136] To ensure the entity had time to make itself compliant, the Minister's request must be in writing, and allow the entity a 28-day grace period in which to become apprised of its obligations as well as the consequences,

---

132 See the *Bill Provisions 2018*, above n 55.
133 Supplementary Explanatory Memorandum, Modern Slavery Bill 2018 (Cth) [1].
134 Commonwealth, *Parliamentary Debates*, Senate, 18 September 2018, 6677–80 (Nigel Scullion).
135 *Modern Slavery Bill 2018*, Proposed Amendments, s 16A(1); Supplementary Explanatory Memorandum, Modern Slavery Bill 2018 (Cth) [11].
136 Supplementary Explanatory Memorandum, Modern Slavery Bill 2018 (Cth) [12].

and make itself compliant or otherwise respond appropriately.[137] In furtherance of that aim, any ministerial request must be accompanied by information about the section of the Act that may result in the entity being publicly identified as non-compliant with a request, along with an assurance that such a decision, which is in effect public shaming, may be subject to merits review.[138]

The non-compliant entity may apply for any number of extensions, and these may be granted, even when made beyond time, although the Minister was not obliged to grant them automatically.[139] If it remains non-compliant after this process, the Minister may publish, on the Modern Slavery Statements Register or any other appropriate way: the entity's identity; its joint or individual failure; details about the extent and duration of its continuing non-compliance (for example dates and details of requests, extensions, and the Minister's determination of the reason the Minister is satisfied that the entity had failed to comply with the requests made).[140]

The second proposed Senate amendment was in line with Labor's fourth proposal made in the House of Representatives, discussed above. It strengthens parliamentary oversight of the implementation of the Modern Slavery Reporting Requirement by adding a new Section 23A to the legislation to require the Minister to report annually to the Parliament.

The Minister's report would be required to include an overview of compliance including trends, general information, numbers of entities publishing statements, and best practice reporting, possibly including entities with best practice statements, and information about current issues.[141]

The third and final proposed Government amendment in the Senate tied any future action on civil penalties to the three-year review, on the basis that, if initial compliance rates were inadequate, penalties might be needed.[142]

The explicit matters to be considered included compliance in the review period, and whether it required additional measures such as penalties to

---

137 Ibid [13].
138 *Modern Slavery Bill 2018*, Proposed Amendments, s 16A(3); Supplementary Explanatory Memorandum, Modern Slavery Bill 2018 (Cth) [15].
139 *Modern Slavery Bill 2018*, Proposed Amendments, s 16A(2); Supplementary Explanatory Memorandum, Modern Slavery Bill 2018 (Cth) [14].
140 *Modern Slavery Bill 2018*, Proposed Amendments, s 16A(4); Supplementary Explanatory Memorandum, Modern Slavery Bill 2018 (Cth) [16].
141 *Modern Slavery Bill 2018*, Proposed Amendments, s 23A(1); Supplementary Explanatory Memorandum, Modern Slavery Bill 2018 (Cth) [24].
142 Supplementary Explanatory Memorandum, Modern Slavery Bill 2018 (Cth) [28].

bring about improvements; whether the Act itself needed to be reviewed, and if so, when; and any other actions needed to improve the regime.[143] This amendment was designed to pin down the issue of penalties and ensure they were considered in light of the way the Act worked without them, along with further reviews of the Act as required.[144]

The Labor Opposition renewed its proposed amendments. These were presented by Senator Farrell.[145] The proposed amendments sustained the Opposition's position on forced marriage (seeking to remove it from the Act in order to focus on it as a separate issue in a different way), as outlined by Tanya Plibersek in the House of Representatives;[146] adding penalties; and requiring the Minister to report annually to the Parliament.[147]

Amendments were also tabled by the Australian Greens (Senator McKim) together with Senator Hinch (Derryn Hinch's Justice Party)[148] and an Independent (Senator Storer), with Senator Hinch and Senator Patrick of the Centre Alliance.[149]

The Greens/Hinch Justice Party amendment related to review of the legislation. It substituted a three-year rolling review.

The Storer/Hinch Justice Party/Centre Alliance proposed amendment was to insert a new Part 3A to establish the office of an Independent Anti-Slavery Adviser, with substantive provisions on appointments and the nature of the office. The Adviser would be required to report annually.[150]

---

143 *Modern Slavery Bill 2018*, Proposed Amendments [7]–[8]; Supplementary Explanatory Memorandum, Modern Slavery Bill 2018 (Cth) [30].
144 *Modern Slavery Bill 2018*, Proposed Amendments [7]–[8]; Supplementary Explanatory Memorandum, Modern Slavery Bill 2018 (Cth) [32].
145 Commonwealth, *Parliamentary Business*, Senate, Committee of the Whole, 2018, Sheet 8549: Amendments to be moved by Don Farrell, on behalf of the Opposition.
146 Requiring amendment to clause 4 of the Modern Slavery Bill: inserting 'other than an offence against Section 270.7B of the *Criminal Code* (forced marriage offences)' to achieve this change.
147 By replacing clause 11 of the Modern Slavery Bill with Labor's preferred version of s 11, and by adding a new s 16A (civil penalties) and 16B (ministerial reporting), as well as a new s 22A (Civil penalty provisions) setting out relevant machinery (authorised applicant, relevant courts, extension to external territories and liability of the Crown).
148 Commonwealth, *Parliamentary Business*, Senate, Committee of the Whole, 2018, Sheet 8519: amendment to be moved by Senator McKim, on behalf of the Australian Greens, and for Senator Hinch, on behalf of Derryn Hinch's Justice Party.
149 Commonwealth, *Parliamentary Business*, Senate, Committee of the Whole, 2018, 8548: amendment to be moved by Senator Storer, and for Senator Hinch, on behalf of Derryn Hinch's Justice Party, and for Senator Patrick, on behalf of Centre Alliance.
150 *Public Governance, Performance and Accountability Act 2013 (Cth)* s 46: (governing annual reporting by the Department) would apply, thus ensuring that the departmental report would include the Adviser's reporting.

4.12 Second and Third Readings

4.12.1 The government's proposed amendments

With only a matter of two or three weeks of sitting days remaining in the 45th Parliament,[151] the Second Reading debate in the Senate resumed on 28 November. The Labor Party, ultimately took the pragmatic approach and accepted the Government's amendments, since not doing so would risk collapse of the legislation entirely. As Senator Pratt (Labor, WA) put it, in commending the Bill to the Senate in the Government's preferred form: 'I think that's a shame ... because there was overwhelming support from stakeholders for some of these changes'.[152]

These sentiments were echoed by the Deputy Leader of the Opposition in the Senate, Senator Farrell (Labor, SA), saying Labor accepted the Government's amendments 'because they improve the Modern Slavery Bill'. They were better than nothing: the Minister had a 'please explain' power, with a 'naming and shaming' process of publishing the details of entities that had failed to comply, but that was a weak solution: big business was being left to police itself, and that was not a good idea, despite the fact that some in business and the broader community had genuine passion to fight slavery. Concerns about compliance by others remained. An 'overwhelming majority' of submissions from stakeholders had called for a penalty regime, and its absence was 'profoundly disappointing'. Labor similarly supported the (again, weaker) requirement that the minister report annually about the operation of the Act, and the three-year review of the regime in operation.[153]

4.12.2 Labor's proposed amendments: forced marriage

Senator Farrell reiterated the reasons his party wanted forced marriage to be removed from the reporting requirements. There were serious concerns about driving the practice underground. Labour reiterated

---

151 On 28 November, after Liberal backbencher Julia Banks announced her departure from the Liberal Party to sit on the cross-bench, the Government announced that it would bring forward the Budget to 2 April 2019, necessarily foreshortening the time available to sit before the federal election. See Prime Minister's press conference: Brett Worthington, *Election Likely for May with Budget Locked in for April, as Morrison's Hold on Power Takes a Hit* (27 November 2018, updated 28 November 2018) ABC News, <www.abc.net.au/news/2018-11-27/election-likely-for-may-as-morrison-locks-in-april-budget/10558080>.
152 Commonwealth, *Parliamentary Debates*, Senate, 28 November 2018, 8920 (Louise Pratt).
153 Commonwealth, *Parliamentary Debates*, Senate, 28 November 2018, 8928.

its 'one-stop-shop' would be introduced if Labour was elected into Government.[154]

The Government's stated reasons for its rejection of Labor's proposal concerning forced marriage were delivered by the Assistant Minister for Home Affairs, Senator Reynolds. The rejection was based, she said, on careful consideration and 'consultation with over 100 expert business and civil society stakeholders' who had 'overwhelmingly supported including forced marriage'. The rationale was that businesses such as mining operations may encourage forced marriage by their practices – for example by setting up 'remote overseas accommodation camps for workers who are forcibly marrying local women'. In addition, religious entities 'may choose to include information in their statements about their actions to ensure that forced marriages do not occur as part of their services'.

The Government's approach was in accord with the Senate Legal and Constitutional Affairs Legislation Committee report, which did not recommend changing the definition of modern slavery.[155]

The Greens' perspective, as outlined by Senator McKim (Tasmania), appeared to be motivated by the belief that removing forced marriage from the umbrella definition in the Bill might diminish its perceived importance and in effect erase it from the class of offences that constituted modern slavery. While the Greens did not support this forced marriage amendment, the wider policy 'would absolutely be something that the Greens could support'.[156] Thus, on the vote, the amendment failed, with 19 'aye' and 38 'no' votes.[157]

4.12.3 Labor's proposed amendments: civil penalties

Senator Farrell repeated Labor's earlier arguments: in short, that business can't be trusted to self-regulate; overseas experience clearly points to the need for penalties;[158] the Act must operate as both a serious

---

154 Ibid (Don Farrell).
155 Ibid 8929 (Linda Reynolds).
156 Ibid 8930 (Nick McKim).
157 Commonwealth, *Journals of the Senate*, 28 November 2018, No. 132, 4307–9: the form of the 'yes' vote is by tradition called 'aye'.
158 Anti-Slavery Australia had provided evidence to the Senate Committee inquiry into the Bill that only about half of the estimate number of organisations required to report in the UK had done so (between 9,000 and 11,000 being required to file a slavery and human trafficking statement): see Anti-Slavery Australia, Submission No. 156 to the Joint Standing Committee on Foreign Affairs, Defence and Trade, *Inquiry into Establishing a Modern Slavery Act in Australia*.

motivator and deterrent for those who would breach it, and that required a 'strong enforcement mechanism' with regulatory teeth.[159]

In reply, Senator Reynolds put forward the Government's position: it rejected the amendments based on business feedback, '[c]ritically, business feedback shows that market scrutiny as well as reputational risk and reward will drive compliance more effectively than punitive penalties'. In answer to the UK issue of whole-scale non-compliance in the first three years, the Government believed the most likely reason for non-compliance over the first three years was implementation difficulties, which acted as a barrier to compliance. Support, not penalties, was therefore in order, and the Government had committed $3.6 million 'to establish a business engagement unit to advise and support businesses through this process'.[160]

In addition, the Government's own amendments (the 'please explain' requirement) would strengthen compliance (largely through 'naming and shaming'); there was now also 'a clear pathway to future penalties' if reviews pointed to the need to introduce them.[161]

Senator McKim, explaining the Greens' reason for supporting Labor's civil penalties, stated that while there was a need to 'work with business', an 'appropriately sized stick' needed to be kept 'in the back of our legislative pocket' to ensure that non-compliance with the Act had consequences.[162]

However, despite these arguments, Labor's proposal to introduce civil penalties also failed on the vote (26 to 29).[163]

4.12.4 The independent Senators' proposed amendments: Anti-Slavery Commissioner and rolling review

Senator Pratt (WA) spoke for Labor in reiterating Labor's support for the independent Senators' proposed amendment[164] to include a new office of Modern Slavery Commissioner. A Business Engagement Unit was insufficient, a Commissioner as a way to achieve real change.[165]

---

159 Commonwealth, *Parliamentary Debates*, Senate, 28 November 2018, 8933 (Don Farrell).
160 Ibid (Linda Reynolds)
161 Ibid.
162 Ibid 8934 (Nick McKim).
163 Commonwealth, *Journals of the Senate*, 28 November 2018, No. 132, 4310.
164 The Storer/Hinch Justice Party/Centre Alliance Amendment.
165 Commonwealth, *Parliamentary Debates*, Senate, 28 November 2018, 8920 (Louise Pratt).

Senator Storer (SA) spoke to the proposed amendment made by himself and Senators Hinch and Patrick (the co-proposers), for an Independent Anti-Slavery Adviser to support the operation of the Act. The adviser would encourage best practice 'in the prevention, detention, investigation and prosecution of modern slavery, and supporting victims'. However, since the Government would not have brought the legislation back before the House of Representatives for further debate, he agreed not to proceed with the proposed amendment.[166] The earlier amendment proposed by the Greens/Hinch Justice Party for a rolling review was also not moved.

4.13 House of representatives Third Reading

The debate being over, the Third Reading proceeded on the motion of Senator Reynolds, with the Government's amendments in place. The Senate then returned the Bill, with amendments, to the House for the final stage of its passage through the House.[167]

On 29 November 2018 in the House of Representatives, the Government's amendments were considered and agreed to immediately, on the motion of Mr Coulton, the Assistant Minister for Trade, Tourism and Investment.[168] The Bill had thus been passed by both Houses in the Government's preferred form, and having passed, it was directed to the Governor-General of Australia for Royal Assent, which it received on 10 December 2018.[169]

---

166 Ibid 8924–5 (Tim Storer).
167 Message No. 475: see Commonwealth, *Votes and Proceedings*, House of Representatives, 29 November 2018, 1988 [17].
168 Commonwealth, *Votes and Proceedings*, House of Representatives, 29 November 2018, 1988 [17]; Commonwealth, *Parliamentary Debates*, House of Representatives, 29 November 2018, 12076.
169 To become Act No. 153 of 2018.

5 International comparisons

5.1 Introduction

Chapters 2–4 provided the background to the *California Transparency in Supply Chains Act 2010*[1] (California Act), the United Kingdom's *Modern Slavery Act 2015, Transparency in Supply Chains provision*[2] (UK Act) and Australia's *Modern Slavery Act 2018* (Cth)[3] (Australia Act).

The Acts require certain entities to have a publicly available modern slavery statement that consumers and the public can scrutinise. The intention is to ensure there is accurate information in the market, to enable consumers, suppliers and other parties to assess, make decisions that support ethical supply chains, and influence good corporate governance.

However, inconsistencies exist between the Acts. This chapter discusses by comparison to the most recent legislative instrument, the Australia Act, these differences.

The California Act applies to retail sellers and manufacturers doing business in California with worldwide gross receipts exceeding USD 100 million. The UK Act covers commercial organisations that carry on business or part of a business in the UK with a total turnover of 36 million pounds and supply goods or services. The Australia Act captures entities based or operating in Australia with AUD 100 million consolidated revenue.

---

1 *California Transparency in Supply Chains Act 2010* passed into law on 1 January 2012. Sections 3 and 4 amended the *California Civil Code 1872* (added § 1714.43) and *California Revenue and Taxation Code 1939* (added § 19547.5).
2 The *Modern Slavery Act 2015* (UK) passed into law on 26 March 2015. The Transparency in Supply Chains provision became operational on 29 October 2015.
3 The *Modern Slavery Act 2018* (Cth) received royal assent on 10 December 2018 and entered into force on 1 January 2019.

Table 5.1 Covered entities

Australia Act	UK Act	California Act
Company	Yes	Yes
Trust	Yes	Yes
Corporate limited partnership	Yes	Yes
Partnership	Yes	Yes
Individual	No	Yes
Bodies politic	No	No
Unincorporated association	Yes	Yes
Superannuation fund	Yes	No
Approved deposit fund	Yes	No

5.2 Covered entities

The Australia Act and the UK Act define what entity types are required to prepare modern slavery statements, thus focusing on the types of business structures that are required to report. Whereas the approach under the California Act is to focus on particular industries and activities (retail seller or manufacturer) without directly specifying the type of business structure required to report within the Act. Here, to ascertain the relevant entity types, reference to other legislative instruments is required.

Common entity types required to report under each Act are companies,[4] trusts,[5] corporate limited partnerships,[6] other

---

4 *Modern Slavery Act* 2018 (Cth) s 4 references 'entity' definition to s 960–100 of the *Income Tax Assessment Act 1997* (Cth) which includes bodies corporate. *Modern Slavery Act 2015* (UK) s 54(12). *Civil Code 1872* (California) § 1714.43(a)(2)(C), (D) references 'manufacturer' and 'retail seller' definitions to *Revenue and Taxation Code* 1939 (California) ('RTC'). RTC § 19 includes companies in definition of 'person' subject to RTC.

5 *Modern Slavery Act* 2018 (Cth) s 4 references 'entity' definition to s 960–100 of the *Income Tax Assessment Act 1997* (Cth) which includes trusts. *Modern Slavery Act 2015* (UK) s 54(12) if trustee is body corporate or a partner in a partnership. *Civil Code 1872* (California) § 1714.43(a)(2)(C), (D) references 'manufacturer' and 'retail seller' definitions to *Revenue and Taxation Code* 1939 (California) ('RTC'). RTC § 19 includes trusts in definition of 'person' subject to RTC.

6 *Modern Slavery Act* 2018 (Cth) s 4 references 'entity' definition to s 960–100 of the *Income Tax Assessment Act 1997* (Cth) which includes bodies corporate. *Modern Slavery Act 2015* (UK) s 54(12) defines 'partnership' to include limited partnerships under the *Limited Partnership Act 1907* (UK). Civil Code 1872 (California) § 1714.43(a)(2)(C), (D) references 'manufacturer' and 'retail seller' definitions to

International comparisons 95

partnerships,[7] and unincorporated associations or body of persons.[8]

The Australia and California Acts further capture individuals,[9] the UK Act does not.[10] As regards bodies politic, the Australia Act only covers such entities.[11] However, in 2018, an Independent Review of the UK Act was undertaken (UK Act Review).[12] In a final report tabled in May 2019, the UK Act Review recommended extension of the UK Act's reporting requirement to the public sector.[13] In July 2019, the UK Government responded to the final report, accepting

---

Revenue and Taxation Code 1939 (California) ('RTC'). RTC § 19 includes limited liability partnerships in definition of 'person' subject to RTC.

7 *Modern Slavery Act* 2018 (Cth) s 4 references 'entity' definition to s 960–100 of the *Income Tax Assessment Act 1997* (Cth) which includes partnerships. *Modern Slavery Act 2015* (UK) s 54(12) defines 'partnership' to include partnerships within the *Partnership Act 1890* (UK) or a firm or an entity of similar character formed under the law of a country outside the UK. *Civil Code 1872* (California) § 1714.43(a)(2)(C), (D) references 'manufacturer' and 'retail seller' definitions to *Revenue and Taxation Code* 1939 (California) ('RTC'). RTC § 19 includes partnerships in definition of 'person' subject to RTC.

8 *Modern Slavery Act* 2018 (Cth) s 4 references 'entity' definition to s 960–100 of the *Income Tax Assessment Act 1997* (Cth) which includes unincorporated associations or body of persons (does not include a non-entity joint venture). *Modern Slavery Act 2015* (UK) s 54(12) defines 'partnership' by reference to the *Partnership Act 1890* (UK). Sections 1 and 2 of this Act define 'partnership' as the relation that subsists between persons carrying on business in common with a view to profit. *Civil Code 1872* (California) § 1714.43(a)(2)(C), (D) references 'manufacturer' and 'retail seller' definitions to *Revenue and Taxation Code* 1939 (California) ('RTC'). RTC § 19 includes associations in definition of 'person' subject to RTC.

9 *Modern Slavery Act* 2018 (Cth) s 4 references 'entity' definition to s 960–100 of the *Income Tax Assessment Act 1997* (Cth) which includes individuals. *Civil Code 1872* (California) § 1714.43(a)(2)(C), (D) references 'manufacturer' and 'retail seller' definitions to *Revenue and Taxation Code* 1939 (California) ('RTC'). RTC § 19 includes individuals in definition of 'person' subject to RTC.

10 An 'individual' is neither a body corporate nor partnership.

11 *Modern Slavery Act* 2018 (Cth) s 4 references 'entity' definition to s 960–100 of the *Income Tax Assessment Act 1997* (Cth) which includes bodies politic. In relation to the California Act, arguably 'bodies politic' do not 'do business' (a pre-requirement imposed by § 1714.43(a)(1) of the *Civil Code 1872* (California) which cross-references § 23101(a) of the *Revenue and Taxation Code 1939* (California) which defines 'doing business' as actively engaging in any transaction for financial or pecuniary gain or profit.

12 Frank Field, Maria Miller, Elizabeth Butler-Sloss, *Independent Review of the Modern Slavery Act 2015, Final Report*, 11 ('*Independent Review*'). See Chapter 3 for further discussion.

13 *Independent Review*, above n 12, 24–5 (Recommendation No. 32).

96 *International comparisons*

this recommendation.[14] A consultation process will determine a range of issues, including the size and type of public sector organisations to report and approval processes.[15]

The Australia and UK Acts both capture superannuation funds[16] and approved deposit funds.[17] The California Act does not extend to these business types, as such entities are not in the business of retail sales or manufacturing.

Table 5.2 Covered sectors

Australia Act	UK Act	California Act
• Goods[18] • Services[19]	• Yes[20] • Yes[21]	• Yes[22] • No

5.3 Covered sectors

The UK and California, in their respective Acts, specify the sectors to which their reporting requirement applies. In contrast, the Australia Act sets out the scope of its reporting requirement in its explanatory memorandum and statutory guidance.

The Australia and UK Acts are broader in their approach, applying to both goods and services, whereas the California Act is limited to tangible goods.

---

14 UK Government, *UK Government Response to the Independent Review of the Modern Slavery Act 2015* (9 July 2019) 11 [39] ('*Government Response to Review*').
15 Home Office, *Transparency in Supply Chains Consultation*, 9 July 2019, 12–13 ('*Transparency in Supply Chains Consultation*').
16 *Modern Slavery Act* 2018 (Cth) s 4 references 'entity' definition to s 960–100 of the *Income Tax Assessment Act 1997* (Cth) which includes superannuation funds. *Modern Slavery Act 2015* (UK) s 54(12) if the trustee of the superannuation fund is a body corporate or a partner in a partnership.
17 *Modern Slavery Act* 2018 (Cth) s 4 references 'entity' definition to s 960–100 of the *Income Tax Assessment Act 1997* (Cth) which includes approved deposit funds. *Modern Slavery Act 2015* (UK) s 54(12) if the trustee of the approved deposit fund is a body corporate.
18 Explanatory Memorandum, Modern Slavery Bill 2018 (Cth) [2]; *Modern Slavery Act 2018 Guidance for Reporting Entities*, (Department of Home Affairs) September 2019, 34.
19 Ibid.
20 *Modern Slavery Act 2015* (UK), s 54(2)(a).
21 *Modern Slavery Act 2015* (UK), s 54(2)(a).
22 *Civil Code 1872* (California), § 1714.43(a)(1).

Table 5.3 Revenue threshold

Australia Act	UK Act	California Act
• AUD 100 million annually[23] • Consolidated revenue[24]	• 36 million pounds annually[25] • Total turnover[26]	• USD 100 million annually[27] • Worldwide gross receipts[28]

5.4 Revenue threshold

The Australia and California Acts set their respective minimum monetary thresholds in their Acts. The UK provides its threshold in regulations.[29]

Whilst each Act has non-equivalent monetary thresholds, each Act is based on global annual amounts. Further, the rationale in each jurisdiction is similar. That is, to capture large entities as such entities have the resources to respond to modern slavery and can exert influence over suppliers to work collaboratively in taking appropriate action.

Notably, the UK Act Review informed that there were 'not many calls' for the turnover threshold to be changed.[30] However, the UK Act Review noted the possibility of reducing this threshold in the future and for the UK Government to keep the turnover threshold under review.[31]

Table 5.4 Modern slavery exploitation forms

Australia Act	UK Act	California Act
• Slavery	• Yes	• Yes
• Servitude	• Yes	• Yes
• Forced labour	• Yes	• Yes
• Deceptive recruitment	• Yes	• Yes
• Forced marriage	• No	• No
• Debt bondage	• Yes	• Yes
• Trafficking in persons and children (all forms)	• Yes	• Yes
• Harbouring a victim	• Yes	• Yes
• Worst forms of child labour	• Yes	• Yes

23 *Modern Slavery Act 2018* (Cth), s 5(1)(a).
24 *Modern Slavery Act 2018* (Cth), s 5(1)(a).
25 *Modern Slavery Act 2015* (UK), s 54(2)(b), (3); *Modern Slavery Act 2015 (Transparency in Supply Chains) Regulations 2015* (UK) SI 2015/1833, reg 2.
26 *Modern Slavery Act 2015* (UK), s 54(2)(b), (3); *Modern Slavery Act 2015 (Transparency in Supply Chains) Regulations 2015* (UK) SI 2015/1833, reg 2.
27 *Civil Code 1872* (California), § 1714.43(a)(1).
28 *Civil Code 1872* (California), § 1714.43(a)(1).
29 *Modern Slavery Act 2015* (UK), s 54(2)(b), (3).
30 *Independent Review*, above n 12, 45 [2.7.2].
31 Ibid.

5.5 Modern slavery exploitation forms

Almost all exploitative forms of modern slavery as defined by the Australia Act are covered across the other jurisdictions, either expressly or indirectly. The Australia Act defines the term 'modern slavery' by reference to other legislative instruments or international treaties.[32] The UK Act defines 'slavery and human trafficking' by reference in part to provisions within the Act,[33] with further clarification in its statutory guidance. The California Act does neither, instead states that 'slavery and human trafficking are crimes under state, federal and international law'.[34]

Common to each of the Acts is: slavery;[35] servitude;[36] forced labour;[37] deceptive recruitment for labour or services;[38] debt

---

32 *Modern Slavery Act 2018* (Cth), s 4 – definition of modern slavery.
33 *Modern Slavery Act 2015* (UK), s 54(12).
34 *California Transparency in Supply Chains Act 2010*, s 2(a).
35 *Modern Slavery Act 2018* (Cth) s 4 references 'modern slavery' definition to *Criminal Code 1995* (Cth), Division 270, which criminalises slavery. *Modern Slavery Act 2015* (UK) s 54(12) defines 'slavery and human trafficking' by reference to s 1 which criminalises slavery. California *Transparency in Supply Chains Act 2010* s 2(a) states 'slavery and human trafficking are crimes under state, federal and international law'. *Penal Code 1872* (California), Pt 1, tit 8, ch 3 Kidnapping, § 207(c) concerns slavery.
36 *Modern Slavery Act 2018* (Cth) s 4 references 'modern slavery' definition to *Criminal Code 1995* (Cth), Division 270, which criminalises servitude. *Modern Slavery Act 2015* (UK) s 54(12) defines 'slavery and human trafficking' by reference to s 1 which criminalises servitude. *California Transparency in Supply Chains Act 2010* s 2(a) states 'slavery and human trafficking are crimes under state, federal and international law'. *Penal Code 1872* (California), Pt 1, tit 7, ch 7 Other Offences Against Public Justice, § 181 concerns involuntary servitude.
37 *Modern Slavery Act 2018* (Cth) s 4 references 'modern slavery' definition to *Criminal Code 1995* (Cth), Division 270, which criminalises forced labour. *Modern Slavery Act 2015* (UK) s 54(12) defines 'slavery and human trafficking' by reference to s 1 which criminalises forced labour. *California Transparency in Supply Chains Act 2010* s 2(a) states 'slavery and human trafficking are crimes under state, federal and international law'. *Penal Code 1872* (California), Pt 1, tit 8, ch 8 False Imprisonment and Human Trafficking, § 236.1(a) concerns forced labour or service.
38 *Modern Slavery Act 2018* (Cth) s 4 references 'modern slavery' definition to *Criminal Code 1995* (Cth), Division 270, which criminalises deceptive recruitment for labour or services. *Modern Slavery Act 2015* (UK) s 54(12) defines 'slavery and human trafficking' by reference to s 2 which criminalises human trafficking. Section 3(5) defines 'exploitation' used in s 2 to include deceptive recruitment for services or benefit. *California Transparency in Supply Chains Act 2010* s 2(a) states 'slavery and human trafficking are crimes under state, federal and international law'. *Penal Code 1872* (California), Pt 1, tit 8, ch 3 Kidnapping, § 207(c) includes false promises and misrepresentation to employ a person.

International comparisons 99

bondage;[39] all forms of trafficking in persons (including children);[40] harbouring a victim;[41] and the worst forms of child labour.[42]

---

39 *Modern Slavery Act 2018* (Cth) s 4 references 'modern slavery' definition to *Criminal Code 1995* (Cth), Division 270, which criminalises debt bondage. *Modern Slavery Act 2015* (UK) s 54(12) defines 'slavery and human trafficking' by reference to s 2 which criminalises human trafficking. Section 3(5) defines 'exploitation' used in s 2 to include deceptive recruitment for services or benefit. Conceivably, this captures debt bondage situations. Further, s 1(2) provides that references to holding a person in servitude is to be construed in accordance with Article 4 of the *Human Rights Convention*. In interpreting Article 4, reference is made to the *Supplementary Convention on the Abolition of Slavery, the Slave Trade and Institutions and Practices Similar to Slavery 1956*. The 1956 Convention identifies debt bondage as a form of servitude. *California Transparency in Supply Chains Act 2010* s 2(a) states 'slavery and human trafficking are crimes under state, federal and international law'. *Penal Code 1872* (California), Pt 1, tit 8, ch 8 False Imprisonment and Human Trafficking, § 236.1(a) concerns forced labour or services. § 236.1(h)(5) defines 'forced labour or services' to mean labour or services through coercion. § 236.1(h)(1) defines 'coercion' to include debt bondage.

40 *Modern Slavery Act 2018* (Cth) s 4 references 'modern slavery' definition to *Criminal Code 1995* (Cth), Division 271, which criminalises trafficking in persons and children for slavery, servitude, forced labour, forced marriage, debt bondage, sexual exploitation, and organ trafficking. Paragraph (c) of the Act also refers to trafficking in persons as defined in Article 3 of the *Protocol to Prevent, Suppress and Punish Trafficking in Persons, Especially Women and Children, supplementing the United Nations Convention against Transnational Organized Crime 2000* ('*Protocol*'). *Modern Slavery Act 2015* (UK) s 54(12) defines 'slavery and human trafficking' by reference to s 2 which concerns human trafficking (adult or child). Section 3 defines 'exploitation' used in s 2 consistent with Article 3 of the *Protocol*. *California Transparency in Supply Chains Act 2010* s 2(a) states 'slavery and human trafficking are crimes under state, federal and international law'. *Penal Code 1872* (California), Pt 1, tit 8, ch 8 False Imprisonment and Human Trafficking, § 236.1(a) concerns human trafficking. § 236.1(g) defines 'human trafficking' to mean 'severe form of human trafficking' in § 7102 of Title 22 of the United States Code. USC, tit 22, ch 78 Trafficking Victims Protection, § 7102(8) defines 'severe forms of human trafficking' as sex trafficking or for involuntary servitude, peonage, debt bondage, or slavery. In relation to organ trafficking, this is prohibited under the *National Organ Transplant Act 1984*.

41 *Modern Slavery Act 2018* (Cth) s 4 references 'modern slavery' definition to *Criminal Code 1995* (Cth), Division 271, which criminalises harbouring a victim. *Modern Slavery Act 2015* (UK) 54(12) defines 'slavery and human trafficking' by reference to s 2 refers to harbouring or receiving a victim. *California Transparency in Supply Chains Act 2010* s 2(a) states 'slavery and human trafficking are crimes under state, federal and international law'. *Penal Code 1872* (California), Pt 1, tit 8, ch 8 False Imprisonment and Human Trafficking, § 236.1(a) concerns human trafficking. § 236.1(g) defines 'human trafficking' to mean 'severe form of human trafficking' in § 7102 of Title 22 of the United States Code. USC, tit 22, ch 78 Trafficking Victims Protection, § 7102(8) defines 'severe forms of human trafficking' to include harbouring a person for labour or services.

42 *Modern Slavery Act 2018* (Cth) s 4 defines 'modern slavery' to include the worst forms of child labour as defined in Article 3 of the *ILO Convention (No. 182) concerning the Prohibition and Immediate Action for the Elimination of the Worst Forms of Child Labour 1999*. *Modern Slavery Act 2015* (UK) in its accompanying statutory guidance refers to the worst forms of child labour (see *Transparency in Supply*

100 *International comparisons*

The Australia Act also captures forced marriage,[43] whereas the intent of the legislation in the UK and California appear not to do so. Of note, is the UK Act Review, which determined that the definition of 'exploitation' in the UK Act was flexible to address new and emerging forms of modern slavery, and as such, no further amendment to the definition was necessary.[44]

Table 5.5 Supply chain

Australia Act	UK Act	California Act
• Beyond direct (tier 1) suppliers[45]	• Ordinary meaning[46]	• Direct suppliers[47]

5.6 Supply chain

Neither of the Acts defines the term supply chain. Instead, the approach by Australia and the UK is to define or provide guidance through secondary materials, primarily statutory guidance.

The Australia Act, through its explanatory memorandum and accompanying statutory guidance expressly defines the term supply chain: 'the products and services (including labour) that contribute to the entity's own products and services. This includes products and

---

Chains etc. A practical guide (Home Office, London 2018), p 18). *California Transparency in Supply Chains Act 2010* s 2(a) states 'slavery and human trafficking are crimes under state, federal and international law'. The *Fair Labor Standards Act* (USA) prohibits oppressive child labour practices in commerce, in the production of goods for commerce, in any enterprise engaged in commerce, or any enterprise engaged in the production of goods for commerce (29 USC § 212(c)). The term 'oppressive child labour' is defined to include employment in jobs and under conditions detrimental to health or well-being (29 USC § 203(l)).

43 *Modern Slavery Act 2018* (Cth) s 4 references 'modern slavery' definition to *Criminal Code 1995* (Cth), Division 270, which criminalises forced marriage.
44 *Independent Review*, above n 12, 27 (Recommendation No. 59).
45 Explanatory Memorandum, Modern Slavery Bill 2018 (Cth) 20 [130]; *Modern Slavery Act 2018 Guidance for Reporting Entities*, (Department of Home Affairs) September 2019, 34.
46 *Transparency in Supply Chains etc. A Practical Guide* (Home Office, London 2018), para 2.2.
47 *Civil Code 1872* (California), § 1714.43(a)(1).

services sourced in Australia or overseas and extends beyond direct suppliers'.[48]

In the UK, statutory guidance refrains from expressly defining the term supply chain, however, does inform that this term is to be given its 'everyday' meaning. This would conceivably imply direct and lower tier suppliers. The UK Act Review recommended legislative amendment to clarify that subject entities must consider the entirety of their supply chains.[49] In its response, the UK Government noted the difficulty in mapping supply chains.[50] In light of this, the UK Government undertook to update the Act's statutory guidance to 'make clear the need for organisations to strengthen their human rights due diligence activities beyond first and second tier suppliers over time'.[51]

In contrast to the approach by Australia and the UK, the California Act refers only to direct suppliers, limiting its reach.[52]

Table 5.6 Disclosure criteria

Australia Act	UK Act	California Act
• Mandatory criteria	• No	• Yes
• Own operations and supply chain	• Yes	• No
• Operations and supply chain of owned or controlled entities	• Yes	• No
• Joint statements	• Yes	• Silent
• Criteria		
• Structure, operations, supply chains	• Yes	• No
• Modern slavery risks	• Yes	• Yes
• Actions to assess and address, including		
• Due diligence	• Yes	• Yes
• Remediation	• Yes	• Yes
• Policy (in note – "may")	• Yes	• Yes
• Training (in note – "may")	• Yes	• Yes
• Assess effectiveness of actions	• Yes	• Yes
• Consultation with subsidiary entities	• Silent	• Silent
• Other information	• Silent	• Silent
• Template	• No	• No

---

48 *Modern Slavery Act 2018 Guidance for Reporting Entities*, (Department of Home Affairs) September 2019, 34.
49 *Independent Review*, above n 12, 24 (Recommendation No. 22).
50 *Government response to review*, above n 14, 9 [28].
51 *Government response to review*, above n 14, 9 [28]. Note, statutory guidance is expected to be updated in 2020.
52 See Chapter 2 for further information on 'direct supply chain' in the California Act.

5.7 Disclosure criteria

The Australia and California Acts have prescribed mandatory criteria.[53] The criteria specified in the UK Act is discretionary.[54] Statutory guidance encourages entities subject to the UK Act to 'aim to include' information in relation to each criteria.[55] The UK and California Acts further permit entities to state, in relation to all or some criteria, that 'no steps' have been taken.[56] This is not a feature of the Australia Act.[57] However, the UK Act Review recommended that the reporting criteria should be mandatory and that the ability to report 'no steps' be removed.[58] The UK Government accepted both recommendations and undertook to consult,[59] with particular concern expressed of the need to 'retain flexibility' so as to allow entities to explain why particular criteria are not addressed. This was premised on the diversity of modern slavery risks across sectors and the varying development stages of reporting entities.[60]

Only under the Australia and UK Acts do entities need to report in relation to both their own operations and supply chains.[61] Both these Acts also require disclosure in relation to the operations and supply chains of any owned or controlled entities.[62] The proviso in the UK Act is if the activities of the subsidiary form part of either the business or supply chains of a parent entity.[63] The approach under the California Act is limited in comparison, with reporting under the California Act only applying in relation to the direct supply chains of a covered entity.[64]

---

53 *Modern Slavery Act 2018* (Cth), s 16(1); Civil Code 1872 (California) § 1714.43(c).
54 *Modern Slavery Act 2015* (UK), s 54(5) uses 'may'.
55 *Transparency in Supply Chains etc. A Practical Guide* (Home Office, London 2018) [5.2].
56 *Modern Slavery Act 2015* (UK), s 54(4)(b); *Civil Code 1872* (California) § 1714.43(c) uses 'if any'.
57 Explanatory Memorandum, Modern Slavery Bill 2018 (Cth), 19 [123].
58 *Independent Review*, above n 12, 23 (Recommendations No. 17 and 18).
59 *Government response to review*, above n 14, 9 [30].
60 *Transparency in Supply Chains Consultation*, above n 15, 7.
61 *Modern Slavery Act 2018 Guidance for Reporting Entities*, (Department of Home Affairs) September 2019 39 [24]. *Modern Slavery Act 2015* (UK), s 54(4) (a)(i) – 'any of its supply chains' and s 54(4)(a)(ii) – 'any part of its own business'. This is also specified in statutory guidance: *Transparency in Supply Chains etc. A Practical Guide* (Home Office, London 2018) [2.3].
62 *Modern Slavery Act 2018 Guidance for Reporting Entities*, (Department of Home Affairs) September 2019 39 [25]. In relation to the *Modern Slavery Act 2015* (UK) this is specified in statutory guidance: *Transparency in Supply Chains etc. A Practical Guide* (Home Office, London 2018), 23.
63 *Transparency in Supply Chains etc. A Practical Guide* (Home Office, London 2018), 23.
64 See Chapter 2 for further information on 'direct supply chain' in the California Act.

International comparisons 103

Joint statements by corporate groups are permitted in Australia and the UK. This is facilitated through statutory provision under the Australia Act and in the case of the UK, through statutory guidance.[65] Both require all entities covered by the modern slavery statement to be clearly identified. In contrast, the California Act is silent on this aspect.

In relation the disclosure areas, again there are similarities and points of difference. The Australia and UK Acts specify a disclosure area concerning an entity's structure, operations and supply chain.[66] Again here, given the scope of the California Act is limited to direct supply chains, this disclosure area is not included in the California Act.[67]

Under all Acts, there is a disclosure area in relation to modern slavery risks,[68] due diligence measures,[69] remediation processes,[70] and assessing effectiveness of actions.[71]

---

65 *Modern Slavery Act 2018* (Cth), s 14(1). In relation to the *Modern Slavery Act 2015* (UK), this is specified in statutory guidance: *Transparency in Supply Chains etc. A Practical Guide* (Home Office, London 2018) [3.4]; *Guidance (online) – Publish an Annual Modern Slavery Statement* (Home Office, 12 March 2019).
66 *Modern Slavery Act 2018* (Cth), s 16(1)(b); *Modern Slavery Act 2015* (UK), s 54(5)(a).
67 See Chapter 2 for further information on 'direct supply chain' in the California Act.
68 *Modern Slavery Act 2018* (Cth), s 16(1)(c); *Modern Slavery Act 2015* (UK), s 54(5)(d). In relation to the *Civil Code 1872* (California), this is specified in statutory guidance: *The California Transparency in Supply Chains Act, A Resource Guide* (California Department of Justice, 2015), p. ii, 11 states in relation to the verification criteria (§ 1714.43(2)(c)(1)) in the *Civil Code* that verifying a product supply chain includes any efforts to identify, assess, and manage the risks of human trafficking in a product supply chain. Accordingly, it is implicit that modern slavery risks ('identify') require disclosure.
69 *Modern Slavery Act 2018* (Cth), s 16(1)(d); *Modern Slavery Act 2015* (UK), s 54(5)(c). In relation to the *Civil Code 1872* (California), this is specified in statutory guidance: *The California Transparency in Supply Chains Act, A Resource Guide* (California Department of Justice, 2015), p. ii, 11 states in relation to the verification criteria (§ 1714.43(2)(c)(1)) in the *Civil Code* that verifying a product supply chain includes any efforts to identify, assess, and manage the risks of human trafficking in a product supply chain. Accordingly, it is implicit that modern slavery due diligence ('assess and manage') is captured. Further *Civil Code 1872* (California) in § 1714.43(2)(c)(2) and (3) refer to audit and certification criteria respectively. Both are forms of due diligence.
70 *Modern Slavery Act 2018* (Cth), s 16(1)(d). In relation to the *Modern Slavery Act 2015* (UK), this is specified in statutory guidance: *Transparency in Supply Chains etc. A Practical Guide* (Home Office, London 2018), 33. This Guide refers to business level grievance mechanisms in its suggested information for the due diligence criteria. In relation to the *Civil Code 1872* (California), this is specified in statutory guidance: *The California Transparency in Supply Chains Act, A Resource Guide* (California Department of Justice, 2015), p. v, 18–19 identifies grievance mechanisms as an internal accountability measure in relation to the internal accountability criteria (§ 1714.43(2)(c)(4)) in the *Civil Code*.
71 *Modern Slavery Act 2018* (Cth), s 16(1)(e); *Modern Slavery Act 2015* (UK), s 54(5)(e). In relation to the *Civil Code 1872* (California), this is specified in statutory guidance: *The California Transparency in Supply Chains Act, A Resource Guide* (California

A point of difference arises in the areas of policy and training. Both the UK and California Acts directly specify these disclosure areas,[72] whereas the Australia Act does not, preferring to include the areas as an example and that too, discretionary.[73]

There is also a point of distinction on the meaning of the term 'effectiveness'. The Australia Act in statutory guidance provides that entities need only report on 'how' effectiveness is assessed.[74] In comparison, the UK Act refers to 'performance indicators' and as such necessitates disclosure not only on the 'how' but also on 'whether' actions to address modern slavery have been effective.[75]

Further, the UK Act Review recommended that entities be required to set out their future due diligence actions.[76] The UK Government accepted this recommendation and committed to updating statutory guidance to 'encourage' future actions.[77]

Only the Australia Act contains a disclosure area that concerns consultation with other entities in preparing a modern slavery statement[78] and other information.[79] Statutory guidance describes 'consultation' broadly (ongoing, meaningful dialogue) and flexibly to allow entities to adopt a process suitable to their circumstances.[80] The 'other category' may include 'good corporate citizen' actions such as contributing to the alleviation of poverty, supporting civil society activities and advocating for legislation in other jurisdictions.[81]

Department of Justice, 2015), p. ii, 11 states in relation to the verification criteria (§ 1714.43(2)(c)(1)) in the *Civil Code* that verifying a product supply chain includes any efforts to identify, assess, and manage the risks of human trafficking in a product supply chain. Accordingly, this definition is broad enough to capture effectiveness in the context of 'managing' modern slavery risks.

72 In relation to policy: *Modern Slavery Act 2015* (UK), s 54(5)(b); *Civil Code 1872* (California) this is specified in statutory guidance: *The California Transparency in Supply Chains Act, A Resource Guide* (California Department of Justice, 2015), p. v, 18–19 identifies codes of conduct as an internal accountability measure in relation to the internal accountability criteria (§ 1714.43(2)(c)(4)) in the *Civil Code*. In relation to training staff: *Modern Slavery Act 2015* (UK), s 54(5)(f); *Civil Code 1872* (California), §1714.43(2)(c)(5).
73 *Modern Slavery Act 2018* (Cth), s 16(1) example; Explanatory Memorandum, Modern Slavery Bill 2018 (Cth) 18 [121].
74 *Modern Slavery Act 2018 Guidance for Reporting Entities*, (Department of Home Affairs) September 2019 54 [70].
75 *Modern Slavery Act 2015* (UK), s 54(5)(e).
76 *Independent Review*, above n 12, 24 (Recommendation No. 20).
77 *Government response to review*, above n 14, 9 [29].
78 *Modern Slavery Act 2018* (Cth), s 16(1)(f).
79 *Modern Slavery Act 2018* (Cth), s 16(1)(g).
80 *Modern Slavery Act 2018 Guidance for Reporting Entities*, (Department of Home Affairs) September 2019 57–58 [83–85].
81 Ibid [145.1].

International comparisons 105

The Australia Act specifies a template for modern slavery statements.[82] The UK and California Acts do not. However, the UK Act Review recommended that the UK Government create a reporting template.[83] The UK Government agreed and committed to updating statutory guidance to include a reporting template.[84]

Table 5.7 Statement approval

Australia Act	UK Act	California Act
• Single statement 　• Principal governing body (PGB)[85] • Joint statement 　• PGB of each entity[86] 　• PGB of higher entity[87] 　• PGB of at least one entity with explanation why other entities not approved[88] • Details of approval 　• Statement that PGB approved[89] 　• Date of approval[90]	• Yes 　• PGB equivalent[91] • Silent • Yes 　• Yes[92] 　• Yes[93]	• Silent • Silent • Silent

---

82 *Modern Slavery Act 2018* (Cth), s 13(2)(b) for single reporting entities and s 14(2)(b) for joint statements.
83 *Independent Review*, above n 12, 23 (Recommendation No. 19).
84 *Government response to review*, above n 14, 8 [26].
85 *Modern Slavery Act 2018* (Cth), s 13(2)(c).
86 *Modern Slavery Act 2018* (Cth), s 14(2)(d)(i).
87 *Modern Slavery Act 2018* (Cth), s 14(2)(d)(ii).
88 *Modern Slavery Act 2018* (Cth), s 14(2)(d)(iii).
89 *Modern Slavery Act 2018* (Cth), s 16(2)(a),(b); *Modern Slavery Act 2018 Guidance for Reporting Entities*, (Department of Home Affairs) September 2019, 64 [12].
90 *Modern Slavery Act 2018 Guidance for Reporting Entities*, (Department of Home Affairs) September 2019, 64 [12].
91 *Modern Slavery Act 2015* (UK), s 54(6)(a) specifies that in the case of a body corporate, the statement must be approved by the board of directors. Section 54(6)(b) states that in the case of a limited liability partnership, the statement must be approved by the members. Section 54(6)(c) provides that in case of a limited partnership under the *Limited Partnerships Act 1907* (UK) the statement must be signed by a general partner. Section 54(6)(d) indicates that for any other kind of partnership, the statement must be signed by a partner. Implicit for (c) and (d) that signing is approval.
92 *Guidance (online) - Publish an annual modern slavery statement* (Home Office, 12 March 2019).
93 Ibid.

5.8 Statement approval

The Australia and UK Acts require approval of modern slavery statements at a senior level. In contrast, the California Act and its statutory guidance is silent on approval of statements.

The Australia Act provides that the principal governing body of an entity must approve its modern slavery statement. This means, a person, body or group of persons responsible for and with control over the entity.[94] Examples include the board of directors in relation to a reporting entity that is a company or in the case of a reporting entity that is a superannuation fund, the board of trustees.[95] The UK Act has equivalent level approval requirements, however, neither the UK Act nor its statutory guidance specifies approval conditions in cases of joint modern slavery statements.

With respect to approval details, both the Australia and UK Acts specify in their respective statutory guidance that a modern slavery statement must expressly state that the statement has been approved by the applicable principal governing body of the entity with an accompanying date of approval.[96]

Of note, is the UK Act Review, which recommended that entities have a 'named, designated board member who is personally accountable for the production of the modern slavery statement'.[97] The UK Government did not accept this recommendation on the basis that approval of modern slavery statements is collective responsibility.[98]

---

94 *Modern Slavery Act 2018* (Cth), s 4 – definition of principal governing body (a). Note, the Act permits rules to be made that may specify the principal governing body for entity types (see (b)).
95 Explanatory Memorandum, Modern Slavery Bill 2018 (Cth) 9 [61].
96 *Modern Slavery Act 2018 Guidance for Reporting Entities*, (Department of Home Affairs) September 2019 64 [12]; *Guidance (online) – Publish an Annual Modern Slavery Statement* (Home Office, 12 March 2019).
97 *Independent Review*, above n 12, 24 (Recommendation No. 24).
98 *Government response to review*, above n 14, 9 [31].

Table 5.8 Statement signing

Australia Act	UK Act	California Act

• Single statement
  • Responsible member (RM)[99]
• Joint statement
  • RM of each entity[100]
  • RM of higher entity[101]
  • RM of entity that approved statement[102]
• Details of signature
  • Name[103]
  • Job title[104]
  • Date[105]
	• Yes
	• RM equivalent[106]
	• Silent
	
	• Yes
	• Yes[107]
	• Yes[108]
	• Yes[109]
		• Silent
		• Silent
		
		• Silent

5.9 Statement signing

Similar to approval of modern slavery statements, signing statements also requires senior level sign-off under the Australia and UK Acts. Again, here, the California Act and its statutory guidance are silent.

Under the Australia Act, a responsible member must sign the entity's modern slavery statement. A responsible member is defined as a member of the principal governing body who is authorised to sign

---

99 *Modern Slavery Act 2018* (Cth), s 13(2)(d).
100 *Modern Slavery Act 2018* (Cth), s 14(2)(e)(i).
101 *Modern Slavery Act 2018* (Cth), s 14(2)(e)(ii).
102 *Modern Slavery Act 2018* (Cth), s 14(2)(e)(iii).
103 *Modern Slavery Act 2018 Guidance for Reporting Entities*, (Department of Home Affairs) September 2019 64 [15].
104 *Ibid.*
105 See approval, 5.8.
106 *Modern Slavery Act 2015* (UK), s 54(6)(a) which specifies that in the case of a body corporate, the statement must be signed by a director. Section 54(6)(b) states that in the case of a limited liability partnership, the statement must be signed by a designated member. Section 54(6)(c) provides that in the case of a limited partnership under the *Limited Partnerships Act 1907* (UK) the statement must be signed by a general partner. Section 54(6)(d) indicates that for any other kind of partnership, the statement must be signed by a partner.
107 Guidance (online) - Publish an annual modern slavery statement (Home Office, 12 March 2019).
108 Ibid.
109 Ibid.

108 *International comparisons*

modern slavery statements.[110] For example, the responsible member of a company is a director. Best practice suggests the head of a principal governing body (Chair of the Board or Chief Executive) sign the modern slavery statement.[111]

The UK Act contains equivalent sign-off requirements to that of a responsible member under the Australia Act. However, here too, neither the UK Act nor its statutory guidance provides sign-off requirements for jointly prepared modern slavery statements.

In relation to sign-off details, both the Australia and UK Acts in their respective statutory guidance set out that the responsible member who signs a modern slavery statement must include their name, position and the date.

Table 5.9 Timeframe for reporting

Australia Act	UK Act	California Act
• Within six months of entity's accounting period or financial year[112]	• Within six months of entity's financial year[113] • Same time as other annual reports[114]	• Silent

5.10 Timeframe for reporting

Both the Australia and UK Acts permit modern slavery statements to be submitted or published within six months of an entity's financial year. Both Acts also provide for alternative reporting timeframes. The

110 *Modern Slavery Act 2018* (Cth), s 4 – definition of responsible member (a). If the entity is a trust administered by a sole trustee the responsible member is that trustee (see (b)). If the entity is a corporation sole, the responsible member is the individual constituting the corporation sole (see (c)). If the entity is under administration, the responsible member is the administrator (see (d)). Note, the Act permits rules to be made that may specify the responsible member for entity types (see (e)).
111 *Modern Slavery Act 2018 Guidance for Reporting Entities*, (Department of Home Affairs) September 2019 64 [17].
112 *Modern Slavery Act 2018* (Cth), s 4 – definition of reporting period; *Modern Slavery Act 2018 Guidance for Reporting Entities*, (Department of Home Affairs) September 2019, 26 [2, 5].
113 *Transparency in Supply Chains etc. A practical guide* (Home Office, London 2018), para 7.4.
114 Ibid.

Australia Act allows statements to be submitted within six months of an entity's accounting period and the UK Act enables statements to otherwise be published at the same time as other annual reports.

In contrast to the flexibility afforded under the Australia and UK Acts, the California Act and its statutory guidance are silent on the issue of reporting timeframes.

The flexibility afforded by the UK Act may change. The UK Act Review did not recommend a single reporting deadline.[115] However, the UK Government, in order to better enable tracking of progress and analysis, is advocating for a single reporting deadline.[116] The UK Government is consulting on various options: 31 March (most UK-registered companies' financial year end); 30 September (six months most UK-registered companies' financial year end); 31 December (the end of the calendar year); 30 June (six months after the end of the calendar year); 30 March for public sector organisations; and 4 April for other types of organisations (in alignment with Gender Pay Gap reporting deadlines).[117]

Table 5.10 Publishing statements

Australia Act	UK Act	California Act

• Central register[118]
  • Freely accessible[119]
  • Public website[120]
• Entity website[121]
	• No
	
	• Yes[122]
	• No website – copy within 30 days[123]
		• No
		
		• Yes[124]
		• Yes[125]

---

115 *Independent Review*, above n 12, 42 [2.3.4].
116 *Government response to review*, above n 14, 10 [33].
117 *Transparency in Supply Chains Consultation*, above n 15, 11.
118 *Modern Slavery Act 2018* (Cth), s 18(1).
119 *Modern Slavery Act 2018* (Cth), s 18(2).
120 *Modern Slavery Act 2018* (Cth), s 18(2).
121 Explanatory Memorandum, Modern Slavery Bill 2018 (Cth) 21 [135].
122 *Modern Slavery Act 2015* (UK), s 54(7).
123 *Modern Slavery Act 2015* (UK), s 54(8).
124 *Civil Code 1872* (California), §1714.43(2)(b).
125 *Civil Code 1872* (California), §1714.43(2)(b).

5.11 Publishing statements

As regards publishing of modern slavery statements, the UK and California Acts adopt the same approach. That is, both Acts require statements to be published on an entity's own website. In the event that an entity has no website, the respective Acts require such entities to provide a hard copy of its statement to any requestor within a 30-day period.

In contrast, the Australia Act establishes a registry that contains all registered modern slavery statements.[126] This register is freely accessible to the public. To enhance consumer transparency, the Australia Act also enables entities to publish their modern slavery statements on their own websites.

Whilst the UK currently has no central registry, this is changing. The UK Act Review recommended the UK establish a publicly accessible and free central register similar to that created under the Australia Act.[127] In response, the UK Government accepted this recommendation and in June 2019, the Prime Minister announced its creation.[128] A consultation process is considering quality indicators and how to incorporate such measurements into the registry.[129]

Table 5.11 Revised statements

Australia Act	UK Act	California Act

• Entity can submit a revised statement[130]
  • Correct errors[131]
  • Update information[132]
  • No time limit[133]
• Include
  • Revision date[134]
  • Changes[135]
  • Address mandatory criteria[136]
  • Approval[137]
  • Sign-off[138]
	• Silent	• Silent

---

126 Under the Australia Act, the Minister has discretion not to register a modern slavery statement that does not meet minimum requirements.
127 *Independent Review*, above n 12, 24 (Recommendation No. 26).
128 *Government response to review*, above n 14, 10 [32].
129 *Transparency in Supply Chains Consultation*, above n 15, 9.
130 *Modern Slavery Act 2018* (Cth), s 20(1).
131 Explanatory Memorandum, Modern Slavery Bill 2018 (Cth) 21 [139].
132 Ibid.
133 Ibid 21 [141].
134 *Modern Slavery Act 2018* (Cth), s 20(2).
135 *Modern Slavery Act 2018* (Cth), s 20(2).
136 *Modern Slavery Act 2018* (Cth), s 20(3).
137 *Modern Slavery Act 2018* (Cth), s 20(3).
138 *Modern Slavery Act 2018* (Cth), s 20(3).

5.12 Revised statements

The Australia Act allows entities to submit revised modern slavery statements. This enables entities to address and correct any false or misleading statements, correct any errors, and if any earlier disclosed information is market sensitive, to accordingly modify such information.[139] Accompanying statutory guidance makes clear that revision of a modern slavery statement has no time period constraints.[140]

A revised modern slavery statement must include the revision date and set out in sufficient detail the changes. Further, the revised statement must address the disclosure criteria and adhere to the previously discussed approval and sign-off requirements under the Australia Act.

The UK and California Acts (or their respective statutory guidance) do not address revised statements.

Table 5.12 Non-compliance

Australia Act	UK Act	California Act
• Minister may request explanation[141] • Minister may request remedial action[142] • Failure to comply with request 　• Minister may publicly identify entity[143] 　• Merits reviewable[144]	• Injunction[145]	• Injunction[146]

---

139 *Modern Slavery Act 2018* (Cth), s 20(1); Explanatory Memorandum, Modern Slavery Bill 2018 (Cth) 21 [139–40].
140 *Modern Slavery Act 2018 Guidance for Reporting Entities*, (Department of Home Affairs) September 2019 65 [26].
141 *Modern Slavery Act 2018* (Cth), s 16A(1)(a).
142 *Modern Slavery Act 2018* (Cth), s 16A(1)(b).
143 *Modern Slavery Act 2018* (Cth), s 16A(4).
144 *Modern Slavery Act 2018* (Cth), s 16A(6).
145 *Modern Slavery Act 2015* (UK), s 54(11).
146 *Civil Code 1872* (California), §1714.43(d).

5.13 Non-compliance

The UK and California Acts adopt the same approach to dealing with non-compliant entities. Both Acts empower injunctive remedial action, by the Secretary of State in the UK and the California Attorney-General for the purposes of the California Act.

In contrast, the Australia Act authorises the Minister to request a non-compliant entity to provide an explanation or perform specified remedial action, or both.[147] The Minister, on the central register or through other means may publicly identify any entity that does not comply with the request. This determination by the Minister is a merits reviewable decision.

Whilst the approach in Australia is different to the UK and California, neither jurisdiction provides for civil penalties for non-compliance. This, in the UK, is proposed to change. The UK Act Review called for a gradual penalty regime. Options recommended included, issuing warning letters (in the first instance), fines (calculated as percentage of turnover), and director disqualification proceedings.[148] In its response, the UK Government agreed with the staggered approach to any penalty mechanism[149] and undertook to consult on the issue. The consultation sets out the Government's preferred option – a capped variable civil penalty (appealable), after a first instance warning letter, with such provision to become operational one year after other amendments to the UK Act.[150]

The UK Act Review, in the context of embedding modern slavery reporting into business culture, also recommended creation of an offence provision in the *Company Directors Disqualification Act 1986* that would apply in instances of failure to report as required under the UK Act or failure to take action in response to a finding or findings of modern slavery.[151] Ultimately, the potential for unintended consequences – statements would likely become high level, led the UK Government to disagree and not accept this recommendation.[152]

---

147 *Modern Slavery Act 2018* (Cth), s 16A(1); Supplementary Explanatory Memorandum, Modern Slavery Bill 2018 (Cth) [8].
148 *Independent Review*, above n 12, 24 (Recommendation No. 30).
149 *Government response to review*, above n 14, 11 [36].
150 *Transparency in Supply Chains Consultation*, above n 15, 9–10.
151 *Independent Review*, above n 12, 24 (Recommendation No. 25).
152 *Government response to review*, above n 14, 10 [34].

Table 5.13 Volunteer entities

Australia Act	UK Act	California Act

• Entities can opt-in[153]
  • Written notice to Minister[154]
  • Single or ongoing period[155]
  • Subject to same requirements as reporting entities[156]
• Entities can opt-out[157]
  • Future reporting periods[158]
	• Yes[159]
	• Silent
	• Silent
	• Silent
	
	• Silent
		• Silent

5.14 Volunteer entities

Australia and the UK Acts allow entities below their respective revenue thresholds to voluntarily comply. The Australia Act enables this in the Act itself, whilst the UK Act provides for this in statutory guidance. The California Act and its accompanying statutory guidance is silent on voluntary compliance.

The Australia Act details a process and condition whereas the UK Act is silent in this regard. Under the Australia Act, entities that wish to comply voluntarily must give notice in writing to the Minister, clearly specifying if their compliance is limited to a single reporting period or for an ongoing basis. Further, the condition set forth is that voluntary entities and subject reporting entities are the same and accordingly must adhere to all requirements in the Australia Act.

The Australia Act also allows entities to opt-out of voluntary compliance. In this circumstance, the entity must give written notice to the Minister. The limitation is that opt-out only applies to future reporting periods, not the current reporting period the entity has previously given notification to comply voluntarily.

---

153 *Modern Slavery Act 2018* (Cth), s 6
154 *Modern Slavery Act 2018* (Cth), s 6(1); Explanatory Memorandum, Modern Slavery Bill 2018 (Cth) 13 [87].
155 *Modern Slavery Act 2018* (Cth), s 6(1).
156 Explanatory Memorandum, Modern Slavery Bill 2018 (Cth) 12 [86].
157 *Modern Slavery Act 2018* (Cth), s 6(3).
158 *Modern Slavery Act 2018* (Cth), s 6(3).
159 *Transparency in Supply Chains etc. A practical guide* (Home Office, London 2018), [3.14].

Table 5.14 List of reporting entities

Australia Act	UK Act	California Act
• No list	• Yes[160]	• Yes, annually[161]

5.15 List of reporting entities

In relation to identifying and compiling a list of reporting entities, the California Act addresses this comprehensively, compared with the Australia and UK Acts.

The California Act requires the California Franchise Tax Board to determine from lodged tax returns entities that are subject to the Act. This is an annual obligation. As regards the UK, the UK Act Review recommended the creation of an internal list, however, individual entities would remain responsible for determining whether they were subject to the UK Act – 'non-inclusion in the list should not be an excuse for non-compliance'.[162] The UK Government accepted this recommendation, noting a list of 17,000 entities had already been compiled.[163]

Australia is currently working towards a list of reporting entities. This follows a recommendation arising from the Senate Legal and Constitutional Affairs Committee report, which examined the provisions of the Australian legislation at the Bill stage.[164]

---

160 *Government response to review*, above n 14, 7-8 [22].
161 *Revenue and Taxation Code 1939* (California), §19547.5(a), (b).
162 *Independent Review*, above n 12, 23 (Recommendations No. 15 and 16).
163 *Government response to review*, above n 14, 7–8 [22].
164 Senate Legal and Constitutional Affairs Committee, *Modern Slavery Bill 2018 [Provisions]*, 24 August 2018 [3.97] Recommendation 1 and [3.98] Recommendation 2. See also Chapter 4 for further discussion on this issue.

Index

Note: **Bold** page numbers refer to tables and page numbers followed by "n" denote endnotes.

Adams, Keren 83
agriculture sector, forced labour in 2
Allain, Jean 33
Annan, Kofi 6
Anti-Slavery Commissioner 68, 91–2; independence of 46, 49; provision for 41; role of 40; Senate Legal and Constitutional Affairs Legislation Committee 78–80
Assembly Appropriations Committee 14
Assembly Judiciary Committee 14
Australia Act: covered entities 94–6, **96**; covered sectors 96, **97**; disclosure criteria 102–5, **105**; modern slavery exploitation forms 98–100, **100**; non-compliance 112–13, **113**; publishing statements 110, **110**; reporting entities list 114; revenue threshold 97, **97**; revised statements 111, **111**; statement approval 106, **107**; statement signing 107–8, **108**; supply chain 100–1, **101**; timeframe for reporting 108–9, **109**; volunteer entities 113, **114**
Australian Labor Party 82
Australian Tax Office (ATO) 78

Bali Process 63, 63n4
Bandt, Adam 84
Bradley, Karen 35, 44, 45, 47

Bribery Act model 36, 37, 42
Brodtmann, Gai 83, 84
Brownley, Saldaña 15, 21
Burrowes, David 43, 45
Business Engagement Unit 79, 84, 91
business-related human rights abuses 5
Butler-Sloss, Baroness 33, 51, 52

CA ACTS Task Force 24, 27
California Act: covered entities 94–6, **96**; covered sectors 96, **97**; disclosure criteria 102–5, **105**; modern slavery exploitation forms 98–100, **100**; non-compliance 112, **113**; publishing statements 110, **110**; reporting entities list 114; revenue threshold 97, **97**; revised statements 111, **111**; statement approval 106, **107**; statement signing 107–8, **108**; supply chain 100–1, **101**; timeframe for reporting 108–9, **109**; volunteer entities 113, **114**
California Civil Code 10
California Franchise Tax Board 114
California Grocers Association 15
California Manufacturers and Technology Association (CMTA) 14
Californian legislation 31, 32, 37–8
Californian regime 34

Index

Californian Senate Bill 657 15–18
California Revenue and Taxation Code 10
California Transparency in Supply Chains Act 2010 8, 10, 48; act in final form 25–9; Assembly amendments 19–25; SB 657 (2009–10) 15–18; SB 1649 (2008) 10–14
Carter, Peter 33, 36, 42
CdeBaca, Luis 34
Centre for Social Justice 30
charity sector 44
child labour, goods produced by 2
Civil Code 16, 20, 29
civil penalties 90–1
Claydon, Sharon 82
CMTA *see* California Manufacturers and Technology Association (CMTA)
Commission to Combat Slavery and Human Trafficking 14, 17, 18, 29
Committee debates (Commons): Eighth and Ninth Sittings 46; First Sitting 41–3; Fourth and Fifth Sittings 45; report stage and Third Reading in 48–9; Second and Third Sittings 43–5; Sixth and Seventh Sittings 46; Tenth and Eleventh Sittings 46–8
Committee on Judiciary 13, 19
Commonwealth's Modern Slavery Act 8n56
Companies Act 43, 46–8, 58
Companies Act 2006 (UK) 36–9
Company Directors Disqualification Act 1986 113
compliance mechanism 68
Connarty, Michael 42, 44, 46
consumer attitudes 59–60
Consumer Federation of California 22–3
Corbett (Senator) 15
Corporate Duty of Vigilance Law (France) 8n56
corporate social responsibility (CSR) 34
Corporate Tax Transparency Report (CTTR) 78
Corporations Act 2001 76
covered entities 94–6, **96**

covered sectors 96, **97**
Cox, Baroness 51
Criminal Code 66, 85
CSR *see* corporate social responsibility (CSR)

Dick, Milton 83
'Died—Assembly—Appropriations' 14
disclosure criteria 102–5, **105**
Draft Modern Slavery Bill 32, 36
Dutch *Child Labor Due Diligence Act* 8n56

Ethical Trading Initiative 44

Fair Trade 36
Farrell (Senator) 88, 89
female: forced labour victims 2; private sector forced labour 1
forced labour victims 2
forced marriage 89–90
Franchise Tax Board 25

Gangmasters legislation 32
Gangmasters Licensing Authority (GLA) 40
General Administrative Order 8n56
Georganas, Steve 83
global supply chains 62–4
Government Code 16, 18, 25, 29
government's proposed amendments 89
Greens/Hinch Justice Party 88
Grocers Association 23

Hamwee, Baroness 51
Hawke, Alex 83
Hinch (Senator) 88, 92
Home Affairs Committee 40
Home Office 30–1, 40
House of Commons 48
House of Lords 56; Committee debates (Lords) 50–4; Second Reading 49–50
House of Representatives 81–5, 92
Howarth, Baroness 51
human rights abuses, remediation for 7
Human Rights Commission 85
human rights standards 3

Index

Independent Anti-Slavery Adviser 88, 92
Independent Anti-Slavery Commissioner 57–60, 63, 70, 84
independent Senators' proposed amendments 91–2
international human rights 6
International Labor Organization, the Declaration 7
international labour standards 7
International Organization for Standardization (ISO) 6
ISO 20400 (Sustainable Procurement) 6
ISO 26000 (Social Responsibility) 6

Johnson, Diana 43, 44
Joint Committee process 32; call for written submissions 32; draft Bill report 36–9; hearings taking evidence in person 33–6
Joint Standing Committee on Foreign Affairs, Defence and Trade (JSCFADT) 62, 63, 65–6; endorsed government's proposed model 66–8; points differs from government's position 68–71

Kearney, Ged 83
Kennedy, Baroness 49

Labor Opposition 88
Labor Party 89
Labor's proposed amendments: civil penalties 90–1; forced marriage 89–90
Lord Alton 49, 52, 54
Lord Bates 52
Lord Deben 52

McKim (Senator) 90, 91
male: forced labour victims 2; private sector forced labour 1
May, Theresa 41n70, 55, 56
modern slavery 1, 62–4
Modern Slavery Act 2015 (UK) 8, 30, 55, 56; Committee debates (Commons) 41–9; consultation and development phase 30–2; final stages and assent 54–5; government's response 39–40; House of Lords 49–54; Joint Committee process 32–9; progression of Bill through Parliament 41; 2018 review 56–61; 2017 proposed amendments 55–6
Modern Slavery Act 2018 (UK) 9, 62; general shape of 71; Interim Report 62–4; JSCFADT 65–71; modern slavery register 73; modern slavery statement 72–3; Parliamentary Joint Committee on Human Rights 74–5, 81; proposed model for public comment 64–5; Second and Third Readings 89–92; Second Reading debate 81–5; Senate consideration 86–8; Senate Legal and Constitutional Affairs Legislation Committee 75–80
Modern Slavery Bill 31, 45, 49
Modern Slavery Bill Evidence Review Panel 31
modern slavery exploitation forms 98–100, **100**
modern slavery reporting requirements 9
modern slavery statements 36–8
Modern Slavery Strategy 50
MSRR Consultation Paper 64, 68
multinational companies: OECD guidelines for 4, 5; remediation for human rights abuses 7

non-compliance, international comparisons 112, **113**
non-compliant entity 87
non-equivalent monetary thresholds 97
nongovernmental organizations (NGOs) 16, 29; anti-slavery work of 30; awareness of modern slavery problem 37; and charities 53

O'Brien, Ted 83
oral evidence 33n17
Organisation for Economic Cooperation and Development (OECD) guidelines, for multinational companies 4, 5

Index

Parliamentary Joint Committee on Human Rights 74–5; information request, Minister's response to 81
Parliamentary Joint Committee on the draft Modern Slavery Bill 32, 34n24, 35n29, 35n31
Patrick (Senator) 88, 92
penalties, Senate Legal and Constitutional Affairs Legislation Committee 76–80
Pérez, John A. 15
Plibersek, Tanya 85, 88
PLS Committee 38
Post-Legislative Scrutiny memorandum 40
Pratt (Senator) 89, 91
pre-legislative stage Committee 31n4
Primark 35
Private Members Bill 56
private sector forced labour 1
Public Bill Committee 41
public list of entities, Senate Legal and Constitutional Affairs Legislation Committee 78, 80
public sector, Government and 59
publishing statements, international comparisons 110, **110**

Regulatory Reform Agenda 64
reporting entities list 114
reporting requirements, development of 8
Revenue and Taxation Code 25, 26, 29
revenue threshold: international comparisons 97, **97**; Senate Legal and Constitutional Affairs Legislation Committee 75–6, 79
Reynolds, Linda 81
Reynolds (Senator) 90–2
risk-based approach 76
Royall, Baroness 51
Ruggie, John 5

Sainsbury 35
SB 657 (2009–10) 15–18
SB 1649 (2008): as amended in Assembly (June 2008) 13–14; as amended in Senate (April 2008) 12; introduction of Bill 10–12
Schwarzenegger, Arnold 10

Scullion, Nigel 86
Second Reading 41; debate, Modern Slavery Act 2018 81–5; House of Lords 49–50
Senate Bill 27
Senate Committee on Appropriations 18
Senate Legal and Constitutional Affairs Committee 114
Senate Legal and Constitutional Affairs Legislation Committee 79–80, 86; Anti-Slavery Commissioner 78–9; penalties 76–8; public list of entities 78; revenue threshold 75–6
Single Labour Market Enforcement Body 59
slavery, definition of 33
Steinberg (Senator) 10, 11, 27
Storer (Senator) 92
Storrer/Hinch Justice Party/Centre Alliance 88
Stunell, Sir Andrew 36, 36n36, 44, 46
supply chains, legislating for 37
supply chain transparency 60–1

Tesco 35
Third Reading: in Committee debates (Commons) 48–9; Modern Slavery Act 2018 (UK) 89–92
'three P' approach 34
Tripartite Declaration of Principles Concerning Multinational Enterprises and Social Policy 7

UK Act 62, 63; covered entities 94–6, **96**; covered sectors 96, **97**; disclosure criteria 102–5, **105**; modern slavery exploitation forms 98–100, **100**; non-compliance 112, **113**; publishing statements 110, **110**; reporting entities list 114; revenue threshold 97, **97**; revised statements 111, **111**; statement approval 106, **107**; statement signing 107–8, **108**; supply chain 100–1, **101**; timeframe for reporting 108–9, **109**; volunteer entities 113, **114**

UK Act Review 95, 97, 101, 102, 104–6, 110, 112, 113
UK-based companies, 'diminished influence' of 40
UK Government: Independent Anti-Slavery Commissioner 60; proposals for an enforcement body 59
UK House of Commons Bill 41
UN Global Compact 6
UN Guiding Principles on Business and Human Rights 5
United Nations General Assembly 6
US Department of Labor 2

Verification, Audit, Certification, Internal accountability and Training (VACIT) 26
voluntary codes 34
volunteer entities 113, **114**

Wallis, Andrew 42, 43
Wilson, Tim 85
World Economic Forum 6
written evidence 33n17